ECOLOGY CRAFTS for Kids

Ecology Crafts for Kids

50 GREAT WAYS TO MAKE FRIENDS WITH PLANET EARTH

BOBBE
NEEDHAM

Sterling Publishing Co., Inc.
New York

A STERLING/LARK BOOK

EDITOR:
BOBBE NEEDHAM

BOOK AND COVER DESIGN:
CHRIS BRYANT

PHOTOGRAPHY:
EVAN BRACKEN

PHOTO STYLIST:
DANA IRWIN

ILLUSTRATIONS:
ORRIN LUNDGREN

PROOFING:
VALERIE ANDERSON

Library of Congress Cataloging-in-Publication Data Available.

10 9 8 7 6 5 4 3 2 1
First Edition

A Sterling/Lark Book

Published by Sterling Publishing Co., Inc.
387 Park Avenue South, New York, NY 10016

Created and produced by Altamont Press, Inc.
50 College Street, Asheville, NC 28801, USA

© 1998, Lark Books

Distributed in Canada by Sterling Publishing
c/o Canadian Manda Group, One Atlantic Avenue,
Suite 105, Toronto, Ontario M6K 3E7

Distributed in Great Britain and Europe by Cassell PLC,
Wellington House, 125 Strand, London WC2R 0BB, England

Distributed in Australia by Capricorn Link (Australia) Pty Ltd.,
P.O. Box 6651, Baulkham Hills, Business Centre, NSW 2153, Australia

Printed in Hong Kong by Oceanic Graphic Printing Productions Ltd.

ISBN 0-8069-0685-5

Thank You's

A VERY BIG THANKS!
to the people and groups who helped with
Ecology Crafts for Kids.

ENTHUSIASTIC KIDS
(AND HELPFUL PARENTS AND FRIENDS)

KELTIE BUCHHOLZ (recycle bin, eco-party)

LACEY BUCHHOLZ (eco-party)

JAMES, SAMUEL, and **THADEAUS CALDWELL** (bottle gardens, potato print shirts, painted pots, eco-hits)

LEIGH AND NATALIE COWART (bat house, sand candles, paper bag bouquets, nature's gardens bottles, eco-adventures)

MARY COWART, mom (sand candles)

NATHAN COX (piñata, recycle bin, marionette, chair, eco-party)

STEVEN DAY (pinch pots)

DANA DETWILER (eco-hits)

WORTH FRADY, friend (bat house)

BEULAH FREEMAN, mom (log cabin planter)

SARAH FREEMAN (log cabin planter, collecting bag, beach glass jewelry, eco-adventures)

KATHY HOLMES, mom (nature journal)

CHRIS MARTIN, great grocery guy

AMY MATHENA, mom (collections box, paper bag books)

IVAN MATHENA (collections box, paper bag books, paper quilts, eco-recycling)

MAGGIE MATHENA (paper bag books, paper quilts, bean and pasta mosaic, eco-recycling)

AMANDA MCGRAYNE (bath salts, paper beads, vegetable paper, hands paper)

IAN MCGRAYNE (dog biscuit frame, vegetable paper, hands paper)

AMANDA MCKINNEY (birdhouse, eggshell mosaic, gourd witch, eco-adventures)

ASHLEY MCKINNEY (birdhouse, gourd witch, beach glass jewelry, eco-adventures)

LLAEL MOFFITT (birch basket, pinch pots, paper bag bouquets, lip gloss, sunflowers, nature's gardens bottles, eco-extravaganzas)

JOSH NOLES (bird feeder, achy breaky pots, nature's gardens bottles, decoupage bottles, rock houses, eco-extravaganzas)

MARY NOLES, mom (bird feeder)

JONATHAN ROBERTS (pinch pots, canoe)

FRENCH SCONYERS-SNOW (achy breaky pots, rock houses, eco-extravaganzas)

FAYE STEVENS (bird, bag bonnets, eco-envelopes, puppets, eco-party)

ANTHONY THOMAS, dad (canoe)

CECE THOMAS (powder, paper quilts, eco-recycling)

TRENTON THOMAS (twig frame, nature's gardens bottles, rock houses, decoupage bottles, eco-extravaganzas)

JESSAMYN WEIS (backyard wetland, nature journal, paper beads)

KARLA WEIS (paper beads)

GRACE WILLIAMS (fish bottle, albums, cabbage rose paper, vegetable paper, hands paper, cornhusk angels)

WHITNEY YOUNG (postcards, bag bonnets, puppets, eco-party)

RACHEL ZITIN (decoupage bottles, albums, cabbage rose paper, hands paper, cornhusk angels)

SPECIAL PHOTOGRAPHERS

Besides our extra-special photographer,
EVAN BRACKEN, *who took nearly all the pictures in this book...*

STEPHANIE AKERS, pelicans, p. 36

CENTER FOR MARINE CONSERVATION, seabird, p.41, and photo by **REX HERRON,** sea turtle, p. 37, both courtesy of the Center for Marine Conservation

BILL DUYCK, chickadee, p. 34; bluebird, p. 36

LISBETH KENT, beach, p. 120

KIDS F.A.C.E. (Kids for a Clean Environment), pp. 22–23

DEBORAH MORGENTHAL, geese, pp. 8, 47

NATIONAL WILDFLOWER RESEARCH CENTER, hedgehog cactus, periwinkle, cactus, pp. 35, 125, 126

BOBBE NEEDHAM, alligators, pp. 8, 11; tree, p. 29; dog, p. 58; newspaper, p. 69; grocery clerk, p. 77

QUALITY FORWARD, pp. 26, 87, 91, 110; mulching, p. 111

RECYCLING KIDS, INC., p. 78

TREE MUSKETEERS, INC., p. 84

TREES FOR LIFE, planting, p. 111

MERLIN D. TUTTLE, Bat Conservation International, pp. 53, 142

U.S. FISH AND WILDLIFE SERVICE, grizzlies, p. 36; buffalo calf, p. 139; and photos by **RONALD L. BELL,** bat, p.52 ; **ASHTON GRAHAM,** whooping crane, p. 37; **ROBIN HUNTER,** humpback whale, p.121 **NASA,** earth from space, pp. 1, 3, 10, 141; **SUE MATHEWS,** bald eagle, p. 35; **B. RATHBURN,** manatee and calf, pp. 8, 61; **TOM S. SMYLIE,** golden eagle, p.122; **BOB STEVENS,** grizzlies, p. 121; **PAMELLA WILSON,** kiln, pp. 16–17

OTHER FINE FRIENDS

THE CENTER FOR MARINE CONSERVATION, a nonprofit group that helps protect marine wildlife and their habitats...**JAN COPE** and **MAYA CONTENTO,** for letting Jessamyn build a wetland in their backyard...**WORTH FRADY,** for the loan of his beautiful flower gardens for photographs... **DANA IRWIN,** for lending most of her family and a generous amount of time to photo shoots...the **NATIONAL WILD-FLOWER RESEARCH CENTER,** a nonprofit group committed to preserving and reestablishing native wildflowers, grasses, shrubs, vines, and trees, and to letting people know how important these are... **QUALITY FORWARD** and **KATIE BRECKHEIMER,** Asheville, North Carolina, for advice and photos; Quality Forward is a nonprofit group of volunteers dedicated to a clean and green community... teacher **LINDA SPERLING,** Erwin High School, Asheville, North Carolina, for letting me visit her class...**TREE MUSKETEERS,** the first eco group founded and run by kids... **KIDS F.A.C.E.** (Kids for a Clean Environment), a kids' environmental group that provides information and project ideas to kids to help them make a positive impact on the environment... **TREES FOR LIFE,** a group that in the United States encourages children to plant trees.

CELTIC BLESSING

DEEP PEACE OF THE RUNNING WAVE TO YOU.
DEEP PEACE OF THE FLOWING AIR TO YOU.
DEEP PEACE OF THE QUIET EARTH TO YOU.
DEEP PEACE OF THE SHINING STARS TO YOU.

CONTENTS

1

Excellent Eco-**EXTRAVAGANZAS**

2

Awesome Eco-**ADVENTURES**

 CALLS FOR ADULT ASSISTANT

Rockin' Eco-RECYCLING

Terrific Eco-TRASH

Happenin' Eco-HITS

Welcome to Ecology Crafts for Kids

Maybe your first question is, What's **ECOLOGY?** You can figure it out yourself.

- ☞ **ECO** *means environment or habitat, the place where a plant or animal usually lives or grows.*

- ☞ **LOGY** *means the science of, or the study of.*

It can't just be the study of habitat, because that would leave out what lives there. So **ECOLOGY** is the study of how plants and animals (including people) interact with where they live...and with each other.

All the plants and animals that live together in one environment form a natural community, called an ecosystem. A lake is an ecosystem. So is a city park. And an ocean. And a desert. And your yard. And a flowerpot.

Does that mean this book is about how to make homes for plants and animals? Not quite. It's about how you can interact in friendly ways with all the living things around you...and with their habitats. About how you can respect everyone's home—Planet Earth—and at the same time have fun making things.

Of course you don't ever mean to harm any creature. You don't go around kicking anthills or pulling down birds' nests. But there are lots of things you can do every day to *help* Planet Earth and all living things. Ecology is a truly awesome adventure.

Do you ever feel like just one person doesn't make much difference in the world? Did you ever want to do something wonderful for the world?

Well, *you're* just one person. And you can make a BIG difference. You are probably already doing wonderful things for the world. You just don't know it.

This book shows you lots of terrific things you can do to be even more of a friend to Planet Earth... and to all the amazing plants and animals who live here with you.

The Projects in This Book

All the projects you can make from this book try to:

- *Use materials that are recycled or reused, or*

- *Use art materials you can find in nature, without harming any habitat or living thing.*

Some things just aren't reusable—you can't reuse glue or paint, for instance. (But you can save leftover paint and use it for something else.) Sometimes you need a certain size of wood, and you don't have scraps that size. But every project tries not to use brand new materials as much as possible.

Reduce. Reuse. Recycle.

You'll see these words a lot in this book. Because they describe what people who want to be friends of Planet Earth do. People like you.

TALKING TRASH

Did you know we are running out of space to put all the stuff we throw away? Three ways to help keep Planet Earth from turning into Planet Trash are **reducing, reusing, and recycling.**

REDUCING

This kind of **reducing** *doesn't mean going on a diet. It means creating less garbage by buying less stuff.*

- I don't know about you, but I buy lots of things I don't really need—like books I could get from the library or birthday cards or gift wrap I could make myself. (And people like homemade things better!)

- An easy way to reduce is to take cloth or net bags with me to the store, instead of using the store's plastic bags—but I often forget!

- Sometimes I buy things I don't even use— I have shirts I've never worn, an electric screwdriver that doesn't work very well, a little tape recorder I've used one time. When I can remember, before I buy something I try to ask myself, Do I really need this? Could I borrow it from a friend? Or could I make it myself?

REUSING

Reusing means saving something I might usually throw away, and using it over again or giving it to someone else to use.

- When I'm finished reading a magazine, I put it in the box at the library for someone to read. I try to reuse plastic bags and glass jars and the blank side of paper. Sometimes I have garage sales—so can you! (Look at page 107 for ideas.)

- Secondhand stores and charity and church groups always want secondhand clothes and toys. Also notebooks, radios, tape players— almost anything. They give them away to people who need them—like homeless people or people whose homes have burned down or been flooded. Or they sell them very cheaply.

- I also buy things at secondhand stores— that's another way of reusing. Check out these stores yourself—you'll find lots of things there for the projects in this book. Also check out flea markets...and garage sales.

- Lots of projects in this book show you great ways to reuse bottles, jars, paper, cans, newspaper, packing material, magazines, paper bags, even old clothes. (You can turn really old clothes into rags.)

Reducing, reusing, and recycling are all easy to do—but sometimes hard to remember to do. A book full of great ideas for you is *50 Simple Things Kids Can Do to Recycle*, by the Earthworks Group. Meanwhile, I'm going to write myself a big sign and stick it on my bathroom mirror: **Reduce! Reuse! Recycle!**

RECYCLING

Of course you know about **recycling** *and why it's so important—mainly so we won't be buried under tons of garbage and make the air so polluted we can't breathe. And also because not recycling wastes trees and energy and metal and oil and raccoons.*

- Raccoons? Yes. And robins, rabbits, rhinoceroses—every wild animal you've ever heard of. Because when we have to bury garbage...or when we cut down trees...or pollute the air by burning trash...we're messing around with the places wild animals live—their habitats.

- Instead of throwing out glass bottles, aluminum cans, paper, corrugated cardboard, soda bottles, and old phone books, I try to remember to put them in my recycling box and take them to the recycling center. If you're lucky, your city picks up your recycled stuff, just like the trash trucks come for your trash.

- If you have a garden or a yard, you can recycle lots of your garbage and yard waste like grass and leaves into plant food, called compost (see page 58). This lets it become part of the life cycle again, instead of buried in a trash heap.

Excellent Eco-EXTRAVAGANZAS

CLAY PINCH POTS AND ANIMALS

Almost nothing is more fun than messing around with clay. You can make something familiar, like these bowls and animals, or a shape totally your own. You may be able to find clay in the bank of a creek or near a place where bricks are made, or you can get it at a craft store. To clean your own clay, see page 15.

WHAT YOU NEED
- A ball of clay as big as your two fists
- A stick or other tool to make designs
- Water

WHAT TO DO

1. Slam the clay down on a big rock or, if you're indoors, on a table covered with newspaper. Pound it, slam it, turn it, pound it, slam it. Keep doing this for about ten minutes—you're getting the air bubbles out of the clay so it won't burst when you fire it in the kiln. This is called *wedging*.

2· Make a ball of clay that you can hold comfortably in your hand. As you hold the clay in one hand, push your other thumb into the middle of the ball almost to the bottom. Keep your thumb there, and very gently and very slowly turn the ball and squeeze the sides between your thumb and fingers as you begin to make a pot.

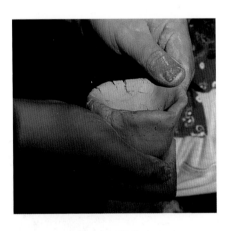

3· Keep turning the pot, and move your thumb up a little at a time toward the top edge, gently pressing as you go to keep the sides of the pot the same thickness. If you see a crack in the clay, rub it gently with a wet finger.

4· Put your pot in a cool place to dry for a day, not out in the sun, which might crack it by drying it too fast. Cover it with a plastic bag.

5· When your pot has dried for one day, you can make designs on it with a stick or other sharp tool.

6· For a special look, when your pot is as hard as leather—not completely dry but not wet—you can burnish it, that is, make it shiny. Rub the surface with a smooth stone or the back of a spoon. After your pot is fired in the kiln, it will be shiny black or brown, like the darkest one in the picture.

TO MAKE ANIMALS

1· Turn a small pinch pot upside down and model it into a frog, an owl, a bear, or any animal you can imagine. Try pushing the top sides up with your thumbs to make frog eyes or owl eyes or bear ears.

2· You can use a sharpened stick, a popsicle stick, or a pencil to press and form legs and feet, eyes, a mouth, or a beak. You might want to make lines for feathers or fur with your stick or pencil.

Cool Tool

FIND AND CLEAN YOUR OWN CLAY

You can buy clay in craft stores, but it's more fun to hunt for it. If you decide to go clay hunting, you need to plan ahead. The clay needs to sit for about two weeks after you find it and clean it before you use it. If you're in a big hurry to make something, you'll probably want to buy your clay.

Two good ways to find clay are to explore around creeks and to follow brick trucks. Unless you're unusually speedy, to follow brick trucks you'll need an adult helper to drive you.

Bricks are made from clay, so trucks that leave brickyards empty are often headed for a big clay deposit to load up. If you ask either at the brickyard or one of the truck drivers, they will usually be glad to tell you where their clay is and let you take some. The white clay pots and animals in this book are made from clay found by following a brick truck (see page 14.)

Around creeks, look along the banks for slippery soil that has nothing growing on it. You can tell it's clay by the feel, and it's usually a different color from the soil around it.

Try to take only as much clay as you will use, so you don't disturb the creek environment any more than you need to.

Cleaning Clay

YOU'LL NEED

- dry clay
- a large sieve or a piece of old window screen nailed to a frame
- a bucket or large pan

First, dry your clay in chunks like those in the photo. Then break the dry clay into small pieces and rub and shake them through the sieve or screen, into the bucket. Throw away any pebbles and sticks—whatever's left in the screen.

Next, add lots of water to your clay and let it sit for a day and a night. It's better to add more water than you think you'll need—it won't hurt the clay. When you can make a long worm with the clay that sticks together well, it's just right. Take the clay out of the water and wrap it in rags to keep it damp.

MAKE YOUR OWN SAWDUST KILN

You can fire your own clay pots, beads, and animals with this kiln—fired clay is much harder and tougher than clay that dries by itself. Your pots will be black or brown or speckled—part of the fun is not knowing exactly what color you'll find. Clay you fire in this kiln will not hold liquid well, so you can use your pots for just about anything but mugs and vases.

Smart Safety Tip:
Have an adult and a bucket of water close by whenever you're working with fire.

Making a Kiln

YOU'LL NEED

- A metal garbage can with a lid
- A hammer
- A big nail or an awl
- A screwdriver
- A bucketful of dry sawdust (from a lumberyard)
- Matches
- Some newspaper
- A bucket of water
- A spray bottle of water
- 12 to 16 bricks
- 4 small chunks of wet clay

1· Find a safe place to build your kiln, outside and away from trees or dry leaves. Bare ground or cement is perfect.

2· Next you punch holes with the hammer and nail. You need four holes about 3" from the bottom of the can, four holes in the middle, and four holes about 3" from the top of the can. Try to make them an equal distance apart around the can. Now twist a screwdriver in the holes to make them about ½" across.

3· Make a circle with four stacks of bricks to go under the can. When you put the can on top, be sure it's steady, not tippy.

4· Now make a sawdust layer 3" or 4" deep in the bottom of the can. Place your pots or other clay you want to fire on top. They should be 2" apart and 4" from the side of the can. Add another 3" of sawdust to cover the pots—be sure to fill the insides of the pots with sawdust too.

5· If you can't fit all your pots in one layer, you can add more sawdust and more layers of pots until the last layer of sawdust is 6" from the top of the can. Now tightly twist about eight sheets of newspaper and place them side by side on top of your last layer of sawdust.

6· Put four chunks of wet clay around the top rim of the can, equal distances apart. These will keep the top from being too tight and will let enough oxygen in to keep your fire burning well.

Smart Safety Tip:
Do not add anymore sawdust to the fire. Sawdust burns very quickly and you could be burned.

7· Light the newspaper carefully. Wait until the fire is burning well and you can see the top of the sawdust before you put on the lid.

8· Gently rest the lid on the chunks of clay. If you put the lid on tight, the fire will go out. If the fire does go out, twist more sheets of newspaper and start the fire over. If the sawdust is burning too fast, spray on a little water to calm it down.

9· Wait for eight to fifteen hours! The time depends on how many things you fired. Check your pots when there is no more smoke coming from the can and when the can is cool to the touch. Carefully lift the lid. All of the sawdust should be gone. In the ashes you'll find your amazing pots or jewelry—who knows what color!

TWIG FRAME

Anywhere trees grow, you can find twigs on the ground—in the park, in your yard, on vacation (maybe not if you go to the beach). You can make frames for your own favorite pictures and frames for special pictures to give to friends. You can frame other things besides pictures, of course—anything you can glue to the cardboard.

WHAT YOU NEED
- Twigs collected from the ground
- Cardboard
- White glue
- Twine, raffia, or string
- Scissors
- A pencil
- A ruler
- A picture

WHAT TO DO

1· To make the back of your frame, figure out how big you want your frame to be and draw the outline on your cardboard with a ruler, then cut it out.

2· Break twigs to the sizes you need for all four sides. You probably want 3 or 4 twigs on each side.

3· Make a bundle of sticks for one side. Wrap twine around each end. Do this for all four sides.

4· Glue your picture on the cardboard. Put plenty of glue on one bundle of sticks and glue it along one side of the picture. Glue the other three sides of the frame.

COLLECTING BAG

HERE'S A GREAT REUSABLE CANVAS BAG TO TAKE ON NATURE WALKS, WHEN YOU'RE OUT COLLECTING SUPPLIES FOR YOUR PROJECTS. AND IT'S PERFECT FOR SHOPPING (TO AVOID USING PLASTIC BAGS)...OR ON CAMPING TRIPS...OR OVERNIGHTS. YOUR DESIGN MAKES IT THE ONLY ONE OF ITS KIND IN THE WORLD.

WHAT YOU NEED
- A canvas tote bag
- A black paint pen
- Acrylic tube paints
- A small, round paintbrush
- Matte medium to thin paints (from craft or art supply stores)
- Masking tape
- Paper and pencil
- A piece of cardboard as big as the bag

WHAT TO DO

1· Tape the cardboard firmly inside your bag. Sketch your design idea on paper, then sketch it on your bag.

2· Paint your design and let it dry.

3· Outline the shapes with the black paint pen.

BIRCH BARK BASKET

YOU CAN MAKE NEAT BASKETS OUT OF NATURAL MATERIALS LIKE VINES, TWIGS, AND BARK. THE MAIN THING TO REMEMBER ABOUT MAKING ANYTHING WITH BARK IS TO GET THE BARK FROM THE GROUND, NOT FROM A TREE. PULLING BARK OFF A LIVE TREE CAN KILL THE TREE, BECAUSE IT LETS INSECTS IN.

WHAT YOU NEED

- Pieces of birch bark and small twigs gathered from the ground
- Bits of moss
- Acorns
- A soup can
- 2 clothespins
- Sharp scissors
- A ruler
- A hot glue gun and glue

WHAT TO DO

1· Cut out pieces of birch bark:
- A piece about 4" wide and 12" long—wide enough and long enough to wrap around your soup can
- A circle about 2½" across for the bottom
- A handle piece about 9½" long and 1" wide

2· Wrap the large piece around the soup can, overlapping the edges at least 1½". Ask an adult to help you with the hot glue gun. Hot glue the edges together. Wrap a few rubber bands around the bark to hold it together while the glue dries.

3· Slide the can out of the basket and glue the bottom on. Press firmly on a table for a few minutes until the glue dries completely.

4· Gently fold the handle and fit it inside the edges of the basket. Hold it in place with clothespins. Remove the clothespins one at a time to hot glue the handle in place. Put the clothespins back on and leave them until the glue dries.

5· Decorate your basket with moss, acorns, and twigs or other natural materials. Hot glue them on.

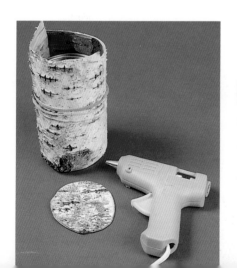

You Can Do It

When Melissa Poe was nine years old, a TV show got her worrying about the environment. She wrote a letter to the president then, George Bush:

Dear Mr. President,

Please will you do something about pollution. I want to live till I am 100 years old. Mr. President, if you ignore this letter we will all die of pollution and the ozone layer.

Please help.

Melissa Poe, Age 9

She also wrote suggestions to newspapers, TV stations, and local politicians. She says that then "I decided to do some of the ideas I had put in the letter, like putting up signs. I first thought about cardboard signs, but then my mom told me about billboards."

Over the next months, Melissa Poe's letter showed up on 250 billboards around the country, including one on Pennsylvania Avenue near the White House where the president couldn't miss it.

EARTH FLAG: *In this photo taken in 1995, the Earth Flag had 20,000 squares handmade by kids, showing their concerns and hopes for the future of the earth. Here it's on display on the Mall in Washington, D.C., to celebrate the 25th anniversary of Earth Day. Kids F.A.C.E. began the flag project—and kept the flag growing.*

Kids F.A.C.E. Gets Going

People began writing to Melissa Poe asking if they could help, or if there was a club kids could join. She started a club called Kids F.A.C.E.—Kids For a Clean Environment. "In the beginning it was just six of my friends," she said. "We did whatever we could, like recycling, planting trees, little things to help."

Then Melissa Poe went on the *Today* show on TV. Kids F.A.C.E. went up to 30 members, then to hundreds, then to thousands.

That was 8 years ago. Melissa Poe is now seventeen. Her club has a budget of $52,000 a year. Kids F.A.C.E. sends out two million copies of their newsletter every two months...gets more than 200 letters a day...has more than 3,000 club chapters in 15 countries...and more than 300,000 members. Membership is free to kids and teachers.

Melissa expects to leave Kids F.A.C.E. soon—it's a kids' club, for kids, by kids. "I want another kid to come along to be the president of the club," she says. "Perhaps someone about 12 who can go and speak in public like I do."

Kids F.A.C.E. members have planted more than 4,000 trees to improve wildlife habitat. They teach other kids and adults about recycling, rainforests, and other environmental issues. They raise money to save the rain forest, help save wildlife...and do whatever they can to help Planet Earth.

SEAL PUP: *Some Kids F.A.C.E. members join the club's Animal Care Team and help out at places like the Marine Mammal Care Center in San Pedro, California. There they might help feed northern elephant seal pups by hand and train them how to catch fish in their natural environment. Or they might help clean tar off baby seals with a mixture of mayonnaise and dishwashing detergent.*

You Can Make a Difference

Melissa Poe says some kids at her school made fun of her at first. "When I was younger, kids would not talk to me at basketball games or they would gang up on me and say, 'Let's get her.' Even today, kids come up to me and say, in a snide way, 'Aren't you that save-the-world girl?'" Maybe they're jealous.

"You can't always think about what other people are going to think of you when you do something," she says. "You have to follow what you think and want to do. When someone says, 'You're just a kid, you can't do that,' I want to prove them wrong. I tell kids that they can do something, that they can get involved and start a club or do something at their school. Don't let anyone tell you that you can't do what you want. As long as you believe that you can make a difference, you can do it."

WANT TO KNOW MORE?
Write to:
Kids F.A.C.E.
P.O. Box 158254
Nashville, TN 37215

TREE-SAVER CHAIR

WHAT YOU NEED

- An old wooden chair
- Sandpaper
- Clean rags
- Leftover latex or acrylic paints
- Used manila folders or thin cardboard
- Paper and a pencil or marking pen
- Rubber glue or double-sided tape
- A small paintbrush or stencil brush
- Urethane sealer or varnish from a hardware department
- A larger brush for the varnish

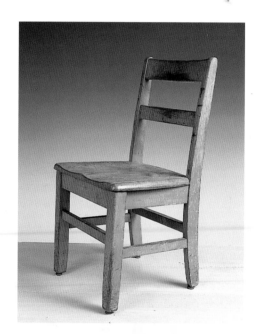

DESIGNING AND PAINTING YOUR OWN CHAIR IS SO MUCH FUN YOU'LL WANT TO MAKE A TABLE TO MATCH...AND A DESK...AND A STOOL. YOU CAN FIND GOOD STRONG OLD CHAIRS AT FLEA MARKETS AND SECONDHAND STORES. YOU MIGHT NOT SAVE A WHOLE TREE BY MAKING OVER AN OLD CHAIR INSTEAD OF BUYING A NEW ONE, BUT YOU'LL SAVE PART OF A TREE. IT ALL ADDS UP...TO A FOREST.

WHAT TO DO

1· Sand all the old varnish or paint off your chair.

24

2· Dip a rag into the paint you want to use for your main color and rub it on the chair. Keep rubbing to let the paint sink into the wood. You can add more paint for a darker color, or use just a little on your rag for a lighter color. Let the chair dry completely. This should take about 14 hours, or overnight.

3· On a piece of paper, draw the designs you want to put on your chair. Plan where each design will go. Copy the designs onto paper the thickness of manila folders. To make stencils, you cut out the part of the design that you want to paint onto the chair. If you want to paint a cross, you cut out the cross. You will paint on top of the paper, and the paint will go through the cross-shaped opening.

4· Stick the first stencil you want to paint tightly to the chair with rubber glue or double-sided tape. You don't want any paint to slide under the paper and mess up your design.

If you have never painted stencils before, you might want to practice a few times on some scrap wood or another piece of paper. Dab on paint with your brush—not too much or it will smear under the stencil. Continue painting stencils on the chair until it looks the way you want it to.

5· When all your stencils are completely dry, you can paint on a coat of urethane sealer or varnish to protect your new paint job.

**Evening came,
and the old fir trees
behind the cottage
began to rustle more loudly
as a strong wind swept along,
roaring among the branches.
Heidi's heart beat faster.
She thought she had never
heard anything so beautiful
and went skipping and running
for sheer joy under the trees.**

—JOHANNA SPYRI, *Heidi*

We'd Be up a Tree without Trees

Trees look like they're just standing around doing nothing most of the time, but they're as important to our ecosystem as humans. Here are some things about trees most people don't know—or don't think about.

▲ In the summertime, one young tree keeps the air as cool as 10 air conditioners going 20 hours a day.

▲ Young trees are our best air purifiers. One acre of young trees uses 5 to 6 tons of carbon dioxide a year—that's 10,000 to 12,000 pounds of the gas that animals and people breathe out. That same acre gives us 4 tons of fresh oxygen to breathe (8,000 pounds).

▲ Around the world, forests provide homes for almost half of all living things.

▲ Maybe your house is built at least partly from trees. Most of the world's buildings are.

▲ This book used to be part of a tree. Trees give us paper, furniture, and lots of other things we use every day.

▲ Trees give us food—apples, peaches, pears, mangos, oranges (you can list lots more fruits)...walnuts, pecans, coconuts, and all kinds of nuts (not peanuts...or doughnuts).

LET'S ROOT FOR TREES! *The average American uses seven trees a year, in paper, wood, and other tree products. These kids are planting cypress trees to make shade, oxygen, and a healthier environment in Asheville, North Carolina. The project sponsor is Quality Forward.*

SPECIAL PRINTS GIFT WRAP

THE GREAT THING ABOUT STAMP PRINTING IS YOU CAN USE THE SAME STAMPS TO DECORATE ALL KINDS OF THINGS—WRAPPING PAPER, BIRTHDAY CARDS, PLACE MATS, WRITING PAPER, T-SHIRTS. TRY DIFFERENT COLORS AND DIFFERENT COMBINATIONS... HAVE FRIENDS OVER AND STAMP IT ON OUT!

WHAT YOU NEED
- Reused paper from mailed packages or paper bags and tissue paper
- Any items with interesting shapes that you can paint
- Idaho potatoes
- A bunch of celery
- Acrylic paints
- Paintbrushes
- A knife (a butter knife is okay)
- Cookie cutters

WHAT TO DO
TO MAKE CABBAGE ROSE PAPER

Cut off the bottom of a bunch of celery. (Store the rest of the celery in the refrigerator to eat.) Paint the bottom of the stalk with acrylic paint and stamp it on tissue paper. If you want to use more than one color, wash off the celery and start over.

TO MAKE HANDS PAPER

Have an old saucer or plastic top for each paint color. Add some water to your acrylic paints, then dip your palm in the paint or paint your hand, then slap your hand onto the paper

TO MAKE VEGETABLE PAPER

1· Cut a potato in half lengthwise. Cut out shapes with a cookie cutter or make up your own shapes. For this vegetable paper, the shapes are a green pea, an eggplant, and a chili pepper.

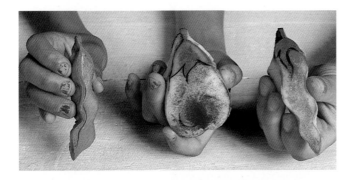

2· Paint your potato stamps and stamp your paper.

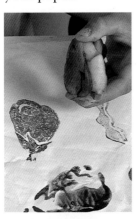

Oh, Christmas Tree!

Did you know that

🌲 Every year for Christmas we cut down enough trees in the United States and Canada to make a forest big enough to cover Rhode Island?

🌲 You can save a tree if you don't buy a cut tree but decorate a live Christmas tree growing in a pot instead?

🌲 You can plant your live Christmas tree in the ground after the holidays and decorate it with food for the birds...or keep it in the pot and use it again next year?

If you don't have a place to plant your living Christmas tree, maybe you can plant it at school or in a friend's yard. Or maybe your city would help you to plant it in a city park.

THE LIVINGEST CHRISTMAS TREE: *A living Christmas tree looks as joyful as a chopped-down tree—maybe more—and you help protect the planet at the same time.*

Bag BONNETS

WHAT YOU NEED

- 2 brown paper grocery bags for each hat
- Paper mache mix in a dishpan or other large pan (see page 70). Wallpaper paste mix works best for these hats.
- Aluminum foil
- Cooking oil
- A bowl that fits your head, for the daisy hat
- A flower pot that fits your head, for the Darth Vader hat
- Scissors
- A flat, smooth surface you can wipe clean

Reuse paper grocery bags and newspaper by creating great hats for costumes, parties, and dress-up. Be a pirate...a fashion model...a cowpoke...a space invader... an alien. Whatever you can imagine, you can make. Invite a friend over for a hat-making party!

WHAT TO DO

1. Mix up plenty of paper mache mix. It will be lumpy and kind of slimy.

2. Cut open the bags at the seams and flatten them out. Then slide one bag into the pan. Make sure to cover all of the paper with mix.

ECO EXTRA: Americans use 50 million tons of paper every year...more than a billion trees' worth.

3· Slide it very slowly out of the pan. It's heavy! Hold it over the pan and gently squeeze the extra mix back into the pan. Then lay the bag carefully on a flat surface and flatten it out. Slide extra mix off with the side of your hand. Repeat this with the second bag.

4· Turn the bowl upside down and smear the outside with plenty of cooking oil. Cover the bowl with a piece of aluminum foil. Then carefully drape the wet bags over the bowl, one at a time.

5· Shape the bags onto the bowl. Fold one side up for the daisy hat. Repeat all of these steps with two other bags for the Darth Vader flower pot hat (except don't turn up the side).

6· When the bags are completely dry, lift the hat forms off the bowl and flower pot.

7· Cut around the edges to make your hats. Decorate with flowers, paint, feathers, or whatever belongs on your hat.

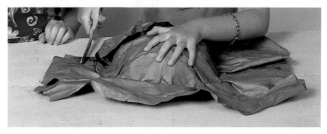

FLY-AWAY-HOME GOURD BIRDHOUSE

ARLY NATIVE AMERICAN INDIANS HUNG GOURDS ON BRANCHES FOR THE BIRDS. THINK ABOUT THAT WHEN YOU HANG UP YOUR GOURD BIRDHOUSE IN THE EARLY SPRING. MAYBE THE BIRDS THAT COME TO YOUR GOURD ARE THE GREAT-GREAT-GREAT-GREAT-GRANDCHILDREN OF THE BIRDS WHO ONCE LIVED IN AMERICAN INDIAN GOURDS. YOU CAN EXPECT TREE SWALLOWS, VIOLET-GREEN SWALLOWS, WRENS, AND CHICKADEES IN THIS BIRDHOUSE.

Smart Safety Tip:
Before you start, ask an adult to help you get the gourd ready for its new owners. The directions are on page 34.

WHAT YOU NEED

- Cleaned gourd with entry hole and drainage holes
- Piece of sponge
- Leftover exterior house paints or acrylic paint—dark green, white, yellow, red
- Old dishes or reused plastic containers to mix paint in
- Small artist's paintbrushes
- String, wire, or leather thong
- Newspaper

WHAT TO DO

1· Tie a piece of string through the top holes so you can hang your gourd up to dry after you've painted it. With the sponge, pat the gourd all over with dark green paint. Cover the whole gourd. Hang it up to dry.

2· Rinse out the sponge. Mix a little white or yellow paint into some dark green paint to make light green. Dip in the sponge and test out some light green patterns on a piece of paper to see what looks good. When the dark green paint is dry, lightly pat the light green paint on the gourd. Let some of the dark green show through. Hang the gourd up to dry.

3· If you want your ladybugs marching in lines, when the light green paint is dry, draw pencil lines for your bugs to march along. Then paint the ladybug bodies on the gourd with red paint. Hang it up to dry.

4· When the red paint is dry, paint on the black ladybug heads. With the tip of a brush, paint a black line down all the ladybugs' backs. Give each bug two black antennae and six black legs. You can make the black ladybug dots with the wooden end of the brush—try this on paper first. Hang the gourd up to dry.

5· When your gourd is dry, hang it up with your string, wire, or leather thong.

CLEANING HOUSE FOR YOUR BIRDS

Before you decorate your gourd, you need to get it in good shape for the birds to move into. For all of these steps, ask an adult to help you.

WHAT YOU NEED
- A dried gourd, about 9" across
- A drill or sharp knife
- Household bleach
- Rubber gloves
- A pot scrubber or brush
- A pencil
- A ruler
- A long-handled spoon
- String or wire for hanging

WHAT TO DO

1· Soak the gourd in a solution of ¼ cup bleach to a gallon of water for half an hour. Put on rubber gloves and scrub the gourd with a pot scrubber. Get it really clean. Then rinse it, dry it, and let it dry in the air for half an hour.

2· Drill or carve small holes about an inch down from the top for hanging.

3· Hang the gourd up to mark the entry hole. The hole needs to be along the outermost curve of the gourd, 4" to 6" above the bottom, pointing straight out—not slanted up or down. Draw a hole 1½" across and 2⅜" high for tree swallows. If you have more chickadees and wrens around your house, draw a hole 1⅛" in diameter. Drill or carve the entry hole.

4· Drill or carve 3 or 4 small drainage holes in the bottom of the gourd, at the lowest point when it is hanging up.

5· Completely clean out the insides of the gourd with the long-handled spoon.

HANGING UP YOUR GOURD HOUSE

Once you have decorated your gourd birdhouse, you want birds to build a nest in it, right? Lots of birdhouses never have birds in them, because someone hangs them up in the wrong place or at the wrong time.

Here are some things you can do so birds will want to build their nest in your birdhouse.

IF YOUR HOUSE IS FOR WRENS, HANG IT:
- 5 to 10 feet off the ground in a tree or under an overhanging roof.
- In early April if you live in the South, in early May in the North.
- Near a brush pile or near lots of bushes, if you can.
- Where it will get some sun.

IF YOUR HOUSE IS FOR CHICKADEES, HANG IT:
- 5 to 15 feet off the ground in a tree. Hardwood trees are best—oak, hickory, maple, beech, walnut, elm, willow.
- In early April in the South, early May in the North.
- Where it gets sun for about half the day.
- With the entrance facing away from the wind, if you can.

IF YOUR HOUSE IS FOR SWALLOWS, HANG IT:
- FOR TREE SWALLOWS, 4 to 5 feet off the ground near a pond, river, or other large water if you can.
- FOR VIOLET-GREEN SWALLOWS, 10 to 15 feet off the ground and under an overhanging roof
- In late February in the South, in late April in the North.
- With the entrance facing away from the wind.

What's a Bald Eagle? What's a Grizzly Bear?

Some day there might not be any more grizzlies or American crocodiles. Or any sea turtles, giant pandas, brown pelicans, or whooping cranes. All of these species, or kinds, of animals and birds are endangered. They are in danger of disappearing from the earth. Not one brown pelican or sea turtle anywhere in the world.

BALD EAGLES, America's national birds, aren't bald...but they are endangered in every state they live in, from Florida to Maine, New York to California.

BLUEBIRDS: Twenty years ago, eastern bluebirds were vanishing fast from the United States. Then people began building special bluebird nest boxes, and hanging them in places bluebirds like to live. They stopped the bluebirds from disappearing. Every person who hung up a bluebird house helped.

BROWN PELICANS (whose beaks can hold more than their belly can) hang out on the fishing pier in Cedar Key, Florida, waiting for handouts. The birds are endangered in most of the places they live, including California, Louisiana, Mississippi, Oregon, Texas, and Washington.

HEDGEHOG CACTUS is one of many endangered U.S. wildflowers. You probably wouldn't pick these—they're too much like porcupines! But it's a good idea not to pick any wildflowers unless you know their species is not in danger of disappearing.

THE MANATEE STAMP (AND OTHERS TOO!):

For three years, third graders at Westfield Area Elementary in Pennsylvania got people to write letters to convince the U.S. Postal Service to create a manatee stamp. In 1996 the U.S. Post Office issued endangered species stamps to remind everyone about endangered wildlife. One of them was a Florida manatee! The other species on the stamps are the black-footed ferret, thick-billed parrot, Hawaiian monk seal, American crocodile, ocelot, Schaus swallowtail butterfly, Wyoming toad, brown pelican, California condor, Gila trout, San Francisco garter snake, Woodland caribou, Florida panther, and piping plover.

• Many kinds of animals, wildflowers, and birds have already disappeared—more than 100 just in the United States. We say they are *extinct*, just like dinosaurs.

• Without help, another 400 species will soon disappear.

• Every week, about 20 species of plants and animals disappear from the world. Don't you wish you could have seen a passenger pigeon or a duck-billed platypus?

The good news is that there are at least 100,000 species of plants and animals left in the United States...and about 14 million in the world. You and I and other people who care can help save endangered species and others that are at risk—about 20,000 in the United States right now.

Humans are the reason most species become extinct. People destroy the places they live, or change those places so much the species die. People cut down forests. They build towns and neighborhoods where plants and animals used to live. They move rivers or dam them up.

What can we do? How can we help save the manatees? How about the Hawaiian monk seals? And the hedgehog cactus?

GRIZZLY BEARS and gulls fish together in Alaska. Grizzlies are endangered in every other state where they live—Colorado, Idaho, Washington, and Wyoming.

LITTER puts many animals and birds in danger. This sea turtle has swallowed a plastic bag it thought was a jellyfish. Sea turtles are endangered everywhere they live, not just because of litter. Many people still eat sea turtles or catch them just for their shells. People have built houses and condos on many of the beaches where sea turtles used to lay their eggs.

WHOOPING CRANES *are almost extinct. In 1941, only 15 were left in the entire United States. Today about 150 are alive, including those in captivity. They live in wilderness wetlands, marshes, and wet prairies.*

What Kids Can Do

TAKE CARE OF YOUR ENVIRONMENTS. Every time you reduce, reuse, and recycle, you're helping save the planet for all living things.. Every time you go outside, you're visiting many creatures' homes. When you walk in a park or the woods, leave flowers and insects and animals where you find them. Leave nests where they are. Respect other living things and their homes.

PICK UP LITTER. Some people remember to take a bag with them when they go for walks, so they can pick up litter. They are wonderful earth-savers. Anytime you're outside and you see litter, pick it up if you can and throw it in the trash or recycle bin. Litter often harms animals and birds.

ADOPT A PIECE OF ENDANGERED LAND. See page 139.

ADOPT A RARE ANIMAL IN A ZOO. Some zoos are trying to save rare animals by making homes for them like their natural habitats. Most zoos let you pick the kind of animal you want to adopt. You send in money to take care of the animal, and the zoo sends you a photo and news of your animal. It could cost as much as $25. You could get friends to help you or have a garage sale or a car wash to make the money.

ADOPT AN ENDANGERED ANIMAL. You can adopt a bison through the Nature Conservancy...a manatee through Save the Manatee...a whale through the International Wildlife Coalition...a dolphin through the EPI Group Limited...an eagle through Conservation International... and many other animals through other environmental groups. Usually you need to send the group some money, and you get a picture and a newsletter and news of your animal. You can find out about these groups at the library or on the Internet. Before you send any money, ask your parents or the librarian to be sure the group is a good one for you to join.

2

Awesome Eco-Adventures

BACKYARD WETLAND

YOU CAN BUILD YOUR OWN SMALL ECOLOGICAL SYSTEM IN YOUR BACKYARD BY PUTTING IN A POND. IF YOU PLACE ROCKS JUST ABOVE THE WATER LINE, BIRDS CAN DRINK FROM IT, AND YOU'RE SURE TO HAVE VISITS FROM RACCOONS, SQUIRRELS, AND FROGS WHO LIVE NEARBY.

After visiting Philadelphia, Louis would fly south with his wife and children so they could see the great savannas where alligators dozed in the swamp water and Turkey Buzzards soared in the sky. And then they would return home to spend the winter in the Red Rock Lakes of Montana, in the lovely, serene Centennial Valley, where all Trumpeter Swans feels safe and unafraid.

—E.B. White, *The Trumpet of the Swan*

WHAT YOU NEED

- A 32-gallon plastic garbage can—green, black, or brown blends in best
- Strong scissors
- A tape measure or ruler
- A shovel
- Large rocks
- Floating pond plants
- Small landscape plants or moss
- Water

WHAT TO DO

1· Trim off the top of the garbage can, so what you have left is 20" high.

2· Find a flat spot and dig a hole that the can will fit in, with about 2" of the top sticking out of the ground.

3· Put the can in the hole, fill it with water, and pack dirt around it if there are any spaces to fill in.

4· Place stones around the rim, and some plants or moss between the stones. Pack dirt tightly around the stones and plants.

5· To take care of your wetland and the wildlife who visit it, scoop out leaves and twigs that fall into it. Keep the water level high, so your visitors can get a drink easily.

The Wet, Wet World of Water

DID YOU KNOW THAT...

• *More than half of your body is water?*

• *Water covers more than three quarters of our planet? (That means for every square mile of land, there are three square miles of water.)*

• *Only a tiny bit of all water on earth is fresh water...and most of that is frozen at the north and south poles?*

So everyone is being careful about taking care of water, right? Wrong. Some kids in New Jersey made a list of all the trash they found along a river near their school. They found tires, socks, a flowerpot, newspaper, cardboard, soda cans, a blanket, lawn chairs, a shopping cart, oil cans, golf bags, shopping bags, roof shingles, and a kitchen sink...and that's not all.

WHAT ABOUT THE OCEAN?

You might think something as big as the ocean can take care of itself. Nope. No matter where you live, the water around you ends up in the ocean...or sometimes in a lake. Creeks and streams run through wetlands and into rivers, and rivers run into the ocean.

So when you hear about endangered species in the wetlands or in the ocean, you can help, even if you've never seen the ocean and live hundreds of miles away.

ALLIGATORS *find a safe home in this protected wetland in Gainesville, Florida.*

HOW CAN YOU HELP?

• *Learn about marine creatures (animals and fish that live in the water)...talk to people about how special they are.*

• *Cut up plastic six-pack carriers before you throw them away—snip each circle with scissors. For some reason, many six-pack carriers end up in the ocean. Sea creatures can get tangled in the rings and strangle or starve.*

• *Use only the water you need for brushing your teeth or washing dishes. Don't let the water just run.*

• *Take short showers instead of baths—it saves water.*

• *If you go fishing, don't throw any trash in the water.*

• *Tell your parents you know how to save up to 5,000 gallons of water a year (this saves money too)! Just fill a gallon plastic bottle with water and put it in your toilet tank.*

• *Collect rainwater for watering your plants and trees. Put a bucket or a barrel outside with a screen over the top.*

A SEA BIRD *confuses ocean trash with food.*

WANT TO KNOW MORE?

A good place to find out more about protecting the ocean and its wildlife is:

**Center for Marine Conservation
1725 DeSales Street, NW
Washington, D.C. 20036**

COLLECTIONS BOX

WHEN YOU BRING HOME THAT GREAT STUFF FROM A CAMPING TRIP OR NATURE WALK, YOU NEED A SAFE PLACE TO KEEP IT ALL...LIKE BLUE JAY AND GOLDFINCH FEATHERS, ROCKS WITH MICA IN THEM, SHARKS' TEETH FROM THE CREEK, ACORNS, SEED PODS, AND ARROWHEADS. YOU NEED A PLACE OF YOUR OWN, WHERE YOU CAN TAKE THEM OUT AND LOOK AT THEM, AND WHEN YOU NEED THEM FOR A PROJECT, YOU KNOW RIGHT WHERE THEY ARE. YOU COULD USE A SPECIAL DRAWER OR SHELF...OR YOU COULD MAKE THIS NIFTY COLLECTIONS BOX BY RECYCLING A CARDBOARD BOX AND MAGAZINES.

WHAT YOU NEED
- 9 large matchboxes (If you need bigger boxes, use shoe boxes. You can use as many boxes as you want to, as long as you have the same number in each layer.)
- A large corrugated cardboard box
- Old magazines, calendars, catalogues, etc.
- Acrylic paints
- A paintbrush
- A sharp knife
- Scissors
- 9 brass paper fasteners or small nuts and bolts
- A glue stick
- Masking tape or cellophane tape
- Some cotton
- A piece of paper with one blank side for labels

WHAT TO DO

1. You can either wait for years, saving up empty matchboxes, or you can empty out nine matchboxes right now. Give the matches to an adult to store in a coffee can or other container with a top.

2. For the front of your drawers, paint one end of each matchbox. Or cut out pictures from magazines and glue them on.

3 For the drawer knobs, ask an adult to help you make a hole in the center of each drawer front with an awl or sharp knife. If you're using brass fasteners for the knobs, stick a fastener in each drawer, and flatten out the legs on the inside to hold it. If you're using nuts and bolts, stick a bolt through each hole and screw on a nut from the inside to hold it.

4 Glue a label on each drawer.

5 Stack your drawers with the same number of drawers in each stack—here we have three stacks of three drawers. Tape each stack together with masking tape or cellophane tape, then tape all the drawers together with the stacks beside each other.

6 Make a cardboard box to fit your drawers. You'll probably need to cut up a bigger box to fit, and tape the sides together. You want your stack of drawers to fit tight in your box. If the whole stack of drawers pulls out of the box when you try to open a drawer, you can glue or tape the stack to the inside of the box.

7 Decorate your box however you want to. You can glue on magazine pictures, like the box here, or glue on any kind of paper, or paint it. You may want to put cotton in some or all of the drawers, if some of your collections are fragile.

BIRCH BARK CANOE

Tired though he was, he climbed a spruce tree and found some spruce gum. With this he plugged the seam and stopped the leak. Even so, the canoe turned out to be a cranky little craft. If Stuart had not had plenty of experience on the water, he would have got into serious trouble with it.

—E.B. White, *Stuart Little*

FIRST, YOU NEED A BIRCH TREE THAT HAS SHED SOME OF ITS BARK. ONCE YOU'VE SEWED UP YOUR CANOE, IT WILL REALLY FLOAT, BUT IT'S NOT WATERTIGHT. NATIVE AMERICAN INDIANS OFTEN SEALED THE SEAMS OF THEIR BIRCH BARK CANOES WITH A MIXTURE OF SPRUCE GUM AND ANIMAL FAT. YOU CAN TRY THAT IF YOU WANT TO, BUT IT'S HARD TO GET THE MIX RIGHT.

WHAT YOU NEED

- A piece of birch bark collected from the ground, large enough to fit the canoe pattern
- Some thin, bendable twigs or vine
- Raffia or fishing line
- A tapestry needle with a large eye
- An awl
- Sharp, strong scissors
- 2 spring-type clothespins
- A hot glue gun and glue
- Paper and pencil
- A bowl of warm water

WHAT TO DO

1· Trace over the canoe pattern on page 46 on another sheet of paper and cut out the pattern. If you want a bigger canoe, you can enlarge the pattern on a copy machine.

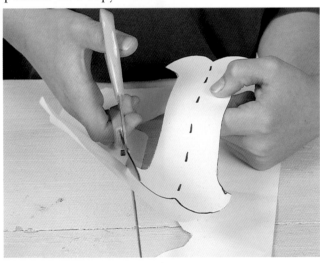

2· Trace the pattern onto your bark and cut out the canoe shape.

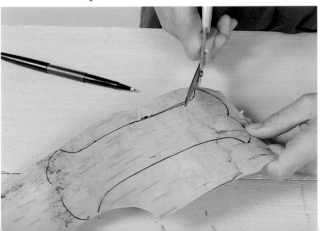

3· Soak your bark in warm water for a moment until you can bend it.

4· Gently bend the sides together and use clothespins to hold the canoe until it dries.

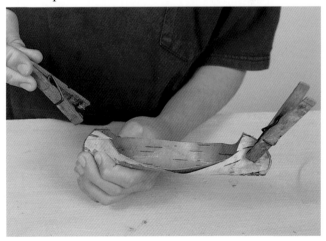

5· Ask an adult to help you hot glue the sides together. Press the glued sides together with clothespins until the glue dries.

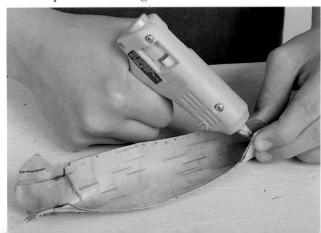

6. Ask an adult to help you make holes with the awl for lacing, along the top sides of the canoe.

7. Thread your needle with the raffia or fishing line. Lay a piece of twig as long as your canoe along the top, so you can lace it to the canoe. Begin lacing at one end and sew up the side at an angle. Then sew back down the same side to create a crisscross pattern. Repeat on the other side.

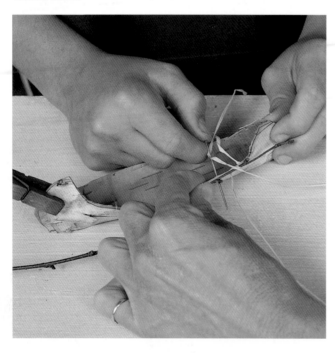

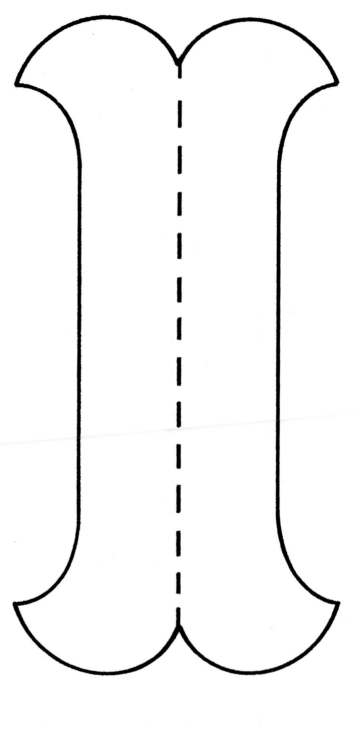

Happy Earth Day!
April 22

The first Earth Day was April 22, 1970—more than 25 years ago. Since then, kids like you all across the United States have worked hard to help protect the earth. They plant trees, recycle trash, and raise money to preserve endangered habitats and species.

- In Hawaii, a Girl Scout troop made an overgrown pond into a wildlife sanctuary. They cleared a path, hauled away trash, and planted native grasses and plants. Now native water birds use the pond again, and volunteer groups keep the habitat safe for wildlife.

- One boy, an Eagle Scout in Illinois, actually created three acres of wetland, a safe home for many birds and plants. He designed the wetland by computer. Then he collected more than 600 plants, and organized other Scouts to help him plant them. He worked with an architect to design and build a boardwalk through the area, with signs explaining wetlands for visitors.

- Elementary school students in Virginia raised money to build a nature trail, with a bridge, benches, and a picnic area. They also included a compost bin and a recycling center.

- Students at a Massachusetts school started a program to recycle lunch waste. They have turned more than four tons of food and paper trash into compost. Students spread the compost in gardens, and they plant flowers all over town.

- A fourth-grade class in Michigan raised money to save a stand of white pine that was about to be cut down. They collected money in their school to "Save a Pine Tree." Then they got other schools involved. They had enough money to save 20 trees. Finally the entire town got interested, and bought the whole 80 acres the trees were growing on...and saved *all* the white pine trees.

KIDS LIKE YOU *help keep creeks, rivers, and lakes clean. In many cities, kids help on "Clean Streams Day" by picking up litter, like these boys cleaning up a section of creek in Asheville, North Carolina.*

CANADA GEESE *and many other birds need clean water and safe wetlands to survive.*

LOG CABIN PLANTER

OF COURSE, IF A REAL LOG CABIN HAD THESE SPACES BETWEEN THE LOGS, THE WIND WOULD BLOW RIGHT THROUGH. BUT THE DESIGN WORKS FINE FOR HOLDING FLOWERPOTS. TO STACK THE LOGS CLOSER TOGETHER, YOU COULD CARVE OUT NICHES IN EACH LOG FOR THE ONES ON TOP OF IT TO LIE IN. YOU CAN ALSO MAKE A FLOOR FOR YOUR PLANTER BY NAILING STICKS ALL THE WAY ACROSS THE BOTTOM.

WHAT YOU NEED
- Twigs collected from the ground, 1/2" to 3/4" across
- Small flat-headed nails
- Pruning shears
- A hammer
- Sandpaper

WHAT TO DO

1· Decide how big you want your planter. If you know what flowerpot you want to put in it, measure that to see how long your sticks need to be. Cut as many twigs as you need, all the same length. (The planter in the photo has 14 twigs.)

2· Choose two twigs with flat sides for the bottom twigs. If they don't lie flat, sand them until they do. You want your planter to be steady when it's finished. Your nails go about 1" in from the ends of the twigs. Hammer nails partway through both ends of both bottom twigs.

3· Hammer nails through the ends of 2 more twigs for the next layer. With the nail points of the bottom twigs pointing up, lay the third twig across the nails (with its nail points pointing up), and hammer it down. Then add the fourth twig, and so on.

4· Keep adding layers of twigs until you have the planter as tall as you want it. Make the top layer extra stable by hammering nails down through the sticks into the layer below, as well as up from the layer below. Put a potted plant on a saucer inside your planter.

Bat House

HUMANS HAVE TAKEN OVER OR DESTROYED LOTS OF PLACES WHERE BATS USED TO LIVE, LIKE ABANDONED BUILDINGS, DEAD TREES, BARNS, AND CLIFFS. SO BATS ARE HAPPY TO FIND WARM, DARK PLACES TO HANG, LIKE THIS BAT HOUSE. THIS IS THE MOST CHALLENGING PROJECT IN THE BOOK— TEAM UP WITH AN ADULT OR TWO WHO HAVE HAD LOTS OF PRACTICE WITH A SAW AND DRILL. WHAT MAKES THIS HOUSE INTERESTING—AND PLANET FRIENDLY—IS THAT IT'S MADE OF OLD BARN WOOD.

ECO EXTRA!
Natural Bug Zappers

One little brown bat eats about 500 insects every hour! The more bats we have flying around chomping on mosquitoes, moths, beetles, stinkbugs, and leafhoppers, the less poisonous insecticides farmers and gardeners will need to use.

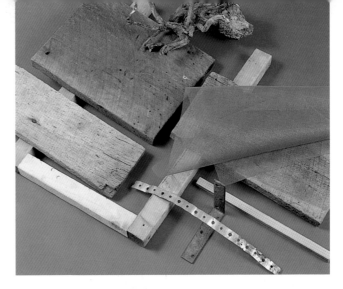

TOOLS AND WOOD YOU NEED

- A handsaw
- A 3/8" electric drill
- 1/8" and 1/4" drill bits
- A #8 countersink
- A hammer
- Clamps
- A Phillips screwdriver
- A tape measure
- Roots or curly branches
  for decoration
- Old wood
  - Roof: 6" x 18"
  - Sides: each 2" x 21½"
  - Top frame: 2" x 11½"
  - Bottom frame: 1" x 11½"
  - Front and back: each 15½" x 21½" (as many
    boards as you need to make the front and
    back the right length and width)

SUPPLIES YOU NEED

- 2¼" decking screws, #8
- ½" staples
- A 15 x 23" piece of old fiberglass window
  screening or ¼" hardware cloth
- ½" wood screws, #4
- Exterior wood glue

WHAT TO DO

1· Cut all the pieces of wood to the right size.

2· Make a box by clamping the sides against the
top frame and the bottom frame. The lower edge
of the frame should be about ½" above the end of
each side. Ask an adult to help you drill. First drill
holes at the corners for the decking screws. Fasten
the box together with glue and decking screws.

☛ **To see if bats have moved into your bat
house, check it twice a month in the summer,
once in fall and winter. When they have lived
there awhile, it won't bother them if you take
a quick peek with a flashlight.**

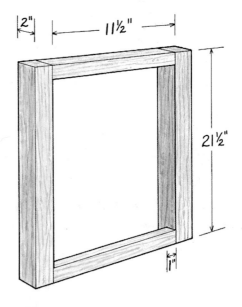

3· Drill ¼" mounting holes through the center of the back pieces that will go at the top and bottom of the frame. Then clamp the back pieces on the frame, centered and even with the ends of each side. Leave a ¾" entrance gap between the back and the bottom frame. Drill 2 holes per board with a #8 drill bit. Fasten with decking screws.

4· On the inside of the house, staple the piece of screen to the back, top frame, and sides. Trim it to fit. The screen helps the bats cling to the inside.

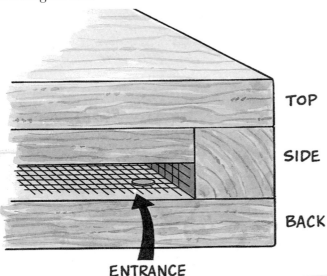

TOP

SIDE

BACK

ENTRANCE

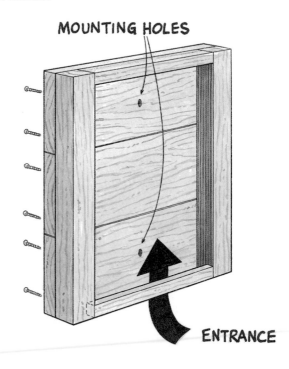

MOUNTING HOLES

ENTRANCE

BAT HOUSE HINTS

In many states, bat species are now endangered, like this Indiana bat. Putting up bat houses in safe places helps bats survive.

- The house needs to get at least 4 hours of sun a day. More sun is even better.

- The higher up the better—at least 12 to 15 feet up on a tree, the side of a building, or a pole.

- If you put your house within a quarter mile of water, like a stream, river, or lake, where there are lots of insects, you are more likely to find bats living in it.

- If you live in a cool or cold climate, paint your bat house a dark color or cover it with tar paper, to absorb and hold heat.

5· Center the front pieces on the frame, even with the upper ends of each side and with the bottom frame.

6· Center the roof on top of the house with its rear edge even with the back. Drill 6 holes with a #8 drill bit. Fasten the roof using glue and decking screws. If you plan to add a flag, use a ¼" bit to drill a ½"-deep hole in the center of the roof.

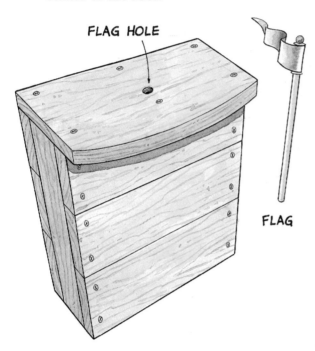

FLAG HOLE

FLAG

7· Add your own ornaments and natural objects to the face of the box, like the curly roots here or bits of found metal.

8· Bats don't like drafts. If the boards of your house don't fit together snugly, seal the spaces with silicone caulk.

Up with Bats!

People have a lot of wrong ideas about bats. For instance... Bats are blind. Bats like to fly into people's hair. Bats have rabies. Vampire bats will suck your blood (yum).

Some facts about bats are:

- Bats can see just fine. But they get around by *echolocation*—they send out squeaks, clicks, and buzzes and listen for the echoes when those sounds bounce off objects in their path, and then they fly around them... so they *locate* things by their *echoes*.

- By echolocation, an ordinary brown bat can detect a human hair three feet away. But like anyone else, bats would rather stay out of people's hair. There's nothing batty about bats.

- Bats do not usually have rabies. But it is important to know that no wild animals like to be caught. If you can catch one, it is probably sick. So it is best not to touch any wild animals, including bats.

- Vampire bats don't attack humans—mostly horses, pigs, and cows, and only in Latin America. They don't suck blood. They bite, then deposit a substance that keeps blood flowing, then lap up the blood. Scientists have just found that the substance in vampire bat saliva that keeps blood flowing is twenty times stronger than anything else like it. Someday this substance may help with serious human problems like heart attacks and strokes.

Up with bats! Be a Batkid!

Help stamp out the silly things people say about bats... spread these important bat truths!

BIG BROWN BATS: *If you live in the United States, you are most likely to have big brown bats come to your bat house—even though there are 40 species of U.S. bats. Big brown bats are about*  *4½ inches long, with wings that open to about 12 inches. Baby bats are born in late May and early June, when big brown bats form nursery colonies of 20 to 300 bats. It takes the young bats only a month to learn to fly.*

 ACHY BREAKY POTS

NEXT TIME SOMEONE AT YOUR HOUSE
BREAKS A PLATE, SAY THANKS, SAVE THE
PIECES (CALLED SHARDS), AND MAKE
ONE OF THESE FANCY FLOWER POTS. OR
RECYCLE A PLATE FROM A GARAGE SALE OR
SECONDHAND STORE. ANYONE WITH A GAR-
DEN HAS OLD CLAY POTS AROUND. ADD A
PLANT, AND YOU'VE CREATED A COOL GIFT.

Smart Safety Tip:
**Always wear safety
glasses when you use tile
nippers. In this project, bits of
the plate might fly up into your
eyes when you're cutting.**

WHAT YOU NEED
- Plates (one or two dinner plates will
  cover the rim of at least one 6" pot)
- Clay pots—scrub dirt off with soap and
  water and allow to dry
- Ceramic tile adhesive and ceramic tile
  grout from a hardware department. (You
  can also use floor or wall grout. Floor grout
  works best if you're leaving large spaces
  between the plate bits. With wall grout you
  must place the plate bits close together.)
- Tile nippers
- A plastic knife or old kitchen knife
- Rags
- An old container for mixing grout
- Newspaper
- Latex gloves
- Safety glasses

WHAT TO DO

1· You only use the edges of your plates. Ask an adult to help you use the tile nippers. Make nips along the edge about ½" to ¾" apart with the tip of the nippers. After you have a pile of pieces, cut them to about ½" wide or as wide as you need them to fit together along the rim of your pot.

2· To glue the cut pieces to the pot, butter the back of one piece with a small amount of tile adhesive, just like you butter toast.

3· Line up the outside edge of each buttered plate piece with the upper edge of the pot and stick it on. Place a second row of pieces under the first row, aligning them with the lower edge of the pot rim. If the pieces don't fit, trim them with the tile nippers, then stick them in place. When both rows are finished, let the pot dry overnight.

4· Squeeze tile grout between the pieces to fill in the spaces. If your grout comes in a can, spread it on with a small rag and push it into the spaces between the shards.

5· Let the grout dry for about 15 minutes, then wipe the surface of the shards clean with a rag. Let the grout dry for about 30 more minutes and wipe the shards clean with a damp rag.

6· Set your pot aside for 2 or 3 days to dry completely. Then you can fill it with soil and plant something in it.

POTATO PRINT SHIRTS

HERE'S A GREAT WAY TO CHANGE AN OLD STAINED SHIRT INTO A FANCY NEW ONE. ANYTHING YOU CAN CARVE INTO A POTATO, YOU CAN PRINT ONTO A SHIRT. ON THE SHIRTS IN THESE PHOTOS YOU'LL FIND FRUIT, VEGETABLES, LEAVES, VINES, BIRDS, A SUN...AND MORE. YOU MIGHT LIKE TO TRY STARS AND MOONS...ANIMALS...LETTERS AND NUMBERS...SOCCER BALLS...OR FLOWERS. OR ALL OF THEM! WHEN YOU'RE FINISHED WITH THE POTATOES, TOSS THEM ON YOUR COMPOST PILE (PAGE 58).

WHAT YOU NEED

- A shirt
- Idaho baking potatoes
- Fabric paint
- A pen
- A paintbrush
- Cookie cutters
- A knife
- Some newspaper

WHAT TO DO

1· Cut some potatoes in half lengthwise. Use a cookie cutter to cut out shapes or draw on your design with a pen and then carve around it. Start with simple ones first, like stars, hearts, suns, and moons. Use a round-edged knife, like a butter knife, to cut away the potato around the design. You want your design to stand up from the rest of the potato, so it will print clearly. Practice until you have some that you like.

2· Lay a few sheets of newspaper flat inside the shirt so the paint won't go through to the other side. Paint the design on the potato with fabric paint.

3· Stamp the potato onto your shirt. When you've finished printing, hang the shirt on a hanger with the newspaper still inside. If you want to print both sides of your shirt, wait until one side is completely dry before you print the other side. Read the instructions on the fabric paint to see if you need to do anything to make the paint permanent before you wash the shirt.

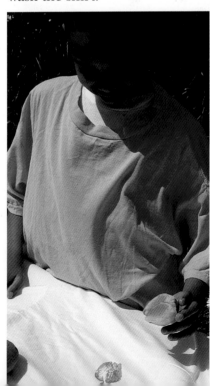

The Great Garbage Mystery

Here's the scene: Your neighbors the Pryors are worried. For the past month, garbage has been disappearing from their kitchen, and it looks like their sweet dog, Pal, must be guilty. They can't find any evidence, like orange peels in his bed, but they think he may have some mysterious disease that makes him hungry for old lettuce, corn husks, and coffee grounds on bread crusts.

Meanwhile, the Pryors have been bragging to you about the healthy new plant their child, Tooperfect, is growing in a big flowerpot on the back porch. But you know Tooperfect pinches Pal when the Pryors aren't around. Yesterday you heard Tooperfect tell Pal, "You're too stupid to understand, but I know where the garbage is going, and I'll never tell. They'll send you away to dog jail. Ha ha ha ha." Then horrible Tooperfect pinched the dog. Hard.

PAL: *Guilty or not guilty?*

With these two clues, you can solve the mystery and save Pal:

1. Tiny creatures called microorganisms live in soil.

2. By breaking food into tiny pieces, microorganisms turn food into fertilizer called compost.

Who has been stealing the Pryors' garbage? Why? Where has the garbage gone? Why doesn't someone pinch Tooperfect?*

The moral of this story is, even someone who recycles food into compost can't be a hero if they still pinch dogs.

*Tooperfect has been stealing the garbage and turning it into compost in the flowerpot, to get Pal into trouble. Why no one has pinched Tooperfect is still a big mystery.

Cool Tool
Make Your Own Compost

To make your own compost, you need a large flowerpot, enough dirt to fill the pot half full, a large plastic bag, and some food scraps. Save up bread crusts, and vegetable and fruit scraps, like banana peels and leftover broccoli and salad. Don't use meat or dairy products like milk and cheese.

Fill the flowerpot about one-quarter full of dirt. Then add food scraps until the pot is about half full. Then cover the food with a thin layer of dirt to keep it from smelling and to keep bugs away.

Put your pot somewhere outside and cover it with the plastic bag. Add a little water to the pot every few days, just to keep it all damp. When you're adding water, stir the mixture up with a large spoon or a spade. The microorganisms need air and water to do their work.

After three or four weeks, most of the food will turn into soil, and soon the food will be entirely gone. You've made compost—fertilizer! Now you can plant a flower in your pot, or you can spoon your compost into the garden or another potted plant and start over.

If your family has a yard or a garden, you can make an entire compost pile. Good places to find out how to make compost piles are your local garden center or your library.

ＳAND CANDLES

HERE'S A USE FOR OLD CANDLE STUBS BESIDES THROWING THEM OUT OR PUTTING THEM IN JACK O' LANTERNS ON HALLOWEEN—JUST AS MUCH FUN, AND YOU CAN USE SAND CANDLES 365 NIGHTS A YEAR INSTEAD OF JUST ONE.

Nature is a sandy dune,
A tall and stately tree,
The waters of a clear lagoon,
The billows on the sea....

—*Jack Prelutsky*

WHAT YOU NEED

- Sand from a beach...from your yard or a road if you live in Florida...or from most garden centers
- Broken candles and candle stubs
- Old crayons
- Bowls, cups, shoes, or any shapes you want to try for molds
- A dishpan, or a large bowl, or a cardboard box lined with a plastic bag
- A spray bottle of water
- An old pan you don't need (or get one from a secondhand store or garage sale)
- An old fork
- A pencil
- A sharp knife
- Newspaper

WHAT TO DO

1· Pour the sand into the dishpan and spray it with water so the hole you make will hold its shape. Then make hollows in the sand with your molds. Or just dig a hole any shape you want to. If you make more than one sand candle at a time in the pan, leave at least an inch of sand between them. Set aside one candle stub for each sand candle—these will provide your wicks.

2· Ask an adult for help with heating and pouring wax. Melt your broken candles and candle stubs in an old pan over medium heat. As the candles melt, carefully dip out the wicks with a fork and lay them on newspaper. If you don't have enough extra stubs for wicks, you can reuse these wicks. Add a crayon stub to dye your candle the color you want.

3· Pour the hot wax into your sand holes.

4· After about five minutes, when the wax starts to get hard, put a candle stub in the center for the wick. If it's too tall, cut it to the right size with a knife. For wide candles, use more than one wick. If you don't have a candle stub, tie one of your used wicks on a pencil and lay the pencil across the top of your hole, so the wick sinks into the center of the candle.

5· Small candles take at least an hour to harden, and bigger ones take longer. Don't try to take yours out of the sand too soon! When your candle is completely cool and hard, gently lift it out of the sand and brush the extra sand off.

Save the Manatee

Manatees are gentle, playful mammals who are friendly to humans. They eat mostly sea plants, but if they get hungry enough they will reach up out of the water to eat from overhanging tree branches. Because they are mammals, they have to breathe. Like dolphins, they can stay underwater for many minutes before they come up for air. Their closest modern relative is...the elephant.

- The average manatee weighs about 1,200 pounds and is 10 feet long. Why would something so big and friendly be endangered? Partly because they're so big and friendly.

- They need lots of food. Human beings have filled up many of the coasts manatees used for feeding grounds. Now they have to go farther to find less food. They also sometimes eat trash, which kills them.

- Most manatees in Florida have scars from being run over by boats. They swim slowly near the surface and don't recognize the danger of boats. In 1991, boats killed 53 manatees, which is about 1 out of every 40 that were alive.

What's the Good News?

In 1981, singer Jimmy Buffet and Florida senator Bob Graham started the Save the Manatee Club to help save manatees from becoming extinct. Some of the things the club does are:

- Help rescue and rehabilitate (cure) manatees

- Put up manatee warning signs in Florida waterways

- Help save critical manatee habitat so manatees can live undisturbed and free.

Through the club, anyone who adopts a manatee gets

- An adoption certificate, a photo, and a biography of their manatee

- A membership handbook with information on manatees

- The Save the Manatee Club Newsletter, four times a year.

Some of the Save the Manatee Club's adopted manatees live at Homosassa Springs State Wildlife Park in Florida. The park is for manatees who are recovering from injuries before being released back into the wild.

HANGING AROUND: *Manatees have been on earth for about 60 million years...and one species, the Florida manatee, has nearly disappeared just in the last 20 years. Only about 2,000 are still alive.*

WANT TO KNOW MORE?
Write to:
Save the Manatee Club
500 N. Maitland Ave.
Maitland, FL 32751, USA

1-800-432-5646

SKETCH-AND-PRESS NATURE JOURNAL

YOU'LL FIGURE OUT LOADS OF WAYS TO USE THIS NATURE JOURNAL. SKETCH IN IT...WRITE ABOUT PLACES YOU GO AND WHAT YOU SEE...TUCK YOUR FINDS UNDER THE RUBBER BANDS...USE IT AS A TEMPORARY NATURE PRESS (PRESS LEAVES, FERNS, OR FLOWERS INSIDE)...PACK IT IN YOUR BACKPACK ON HIKING AND CAMPING TRIPS. YOU CAN MAKE IT ANY SIZE—WHATEVER WORKS BEST FOR YOU!

WHAT YOU NEED

- Cardboard from used corrugated boxes
- Rubber bands
- White glue
- Packing, duct, or electrical tape
- Cellophane tape
- 4 machine screws (1" or 1¹/2")
- 4 hex or wing nuts
- 8 washers
- Recycled paper
- A hole punch
- An awl
- A ruler
- Scissors
- A craft knife
- A pencil

WHAT TO DO

First, figure out how big you want your journal. The measurements here are for a journal that fits 8½" by 14" paper.

1· Measure a large piece of cardboard into 4 pieces that are each 8½" by 14".

2· Ask an adult to help with cutting and using the awl. Cut the pieces of cardboard with a craft knife or other sharp knife.

3· Glue two of the pieces together with white glue. Fit the pieces together, press them together, and put books on top of them overnight to be sure they stick together well.

4· Cut one of the other pieces in half, so you'll have two pieces that are 8½" by 7" for the covers. Measure and mark a line 1½" in from the side of both cover pieces.

5· Cut along the lines with a craft knife.

6· Tape the cover pieces to the 8½" by 14" back with a small piece of cellophane tape.

7· To make hinges so the front covers will bend, wrap duct or packing tape around each cover and the back in one long piece on each side.

8· Hold the back and front cover pieces together with rubber bands. Mark where you want to put the machine screws. With the awl, make small holes for the machine screws.

Ants' ways, beetles' ways, bees' ways, frogs' ways, birds' ways, plants' ways, gave him a new world to explore and when Dickon revealed them all and added foxes' ways, otters' ways, ferrets' ways, squirrels' ways, and trouts' and water-rats' and badgers' ways, there was no end to the things to talk about and think over.

—Frances Hodgson Burnett, *The Secret Garden*

9· Put one sheet of paper under the back and mark with a pencil where the holes for the machine screws belong. Use a hole punch to punch holes in as much paper as you want to use.

10· To put the book together, thread a washer onto a machine screw and insert the screw from the back. Do this for each hole. Then put on the paper, then the top cover, then another washer and a nut or wing nut.

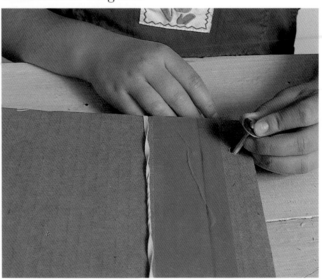

COOL TOOL

Keep a Tree Diary

Many gardeners keep records of their gardens. They write down when they plant, what happens, what kind of weather they had, and so on. Maybe you would like to keep a record of the trees you plant, something like the one here. You could keep it in your nature journal (see page 62) or make a paper bag book for it (see page 73). You could also take photographs of your trees as they grow.

You might write something like this:

My tree is an American dogwood. Its scientific name is C. florida. It could grow to be 40 feet tall with a trunk about 18 inches around.

I planted my dogwood sapling on September 1, 1998. It was 36 inches tall.

Interesting facts about my tree:

1. There are 40 kinds of dogwood. 14 kinds are native to the U.S. and Canada.

2. It is the state flower or tree of North Carolina, Missouri, Virginia, and British Columbia.

3. It is my favorite kind of tree. My grandmother has a pink dogwood in her yard, but mine will have white flowers.

What I will do differently next time:

Plant more than one sapling at the same time, in case something happens to one of them.

My Tree Diary

My tree is a _____ tree.

Its scientific name is _____.

It could grow to be _____ feet tall with a trunk about _____ inches around.

I planted my _____ on _____.
(DATE)
It was _____ inches tall. (Or I planted my _____ seeds on _____.
(DATE)
I first saw my sapling on _____. I planted my tree in the earth on_____ when
(DATE)
it was _____ inches tall.)

Interesting facts about my tree:

What I will do differently next time:

3

Rockin' Eco-Recycling

LIGHT BULB PUPPETS

RECYCLE LIGHT BULBS, NEWSPAPER, FOOD CONTAINERS, AND GROCERY BAGS TO MAKE PUPPETS THAT WILL LIGHT UP ANY STAGE. TRY COUNT DRACULA AND THE RED QUEEN, OR DREAM UP YOUR OWN PUPPET PEOPLE.

WHAT YOU NEED (FOR TWO PUPPETS)

- Two burned-out light bulbs
- A small cottage cheese container
- A small yogurt or sour cream container
- Used brown paper grocery bags
- Used aluminum foil
- Poster paints
- A paintbrush
- A sharp knife
- A pencil
- Scissors
- Tape
- Paper mache mix (see page 70)

WHAT TO DO

Make paper mache mix. For this project, white glue mix works well. Make a pile of pieces of newspaper about ½" by 1".

TO MAKE THE HEADS

1· Cover just the glass part of your light bulbs with aluminum foil. Leave the screw part of the bulb sticking out. Pinch the foil to shape the puppet nose, ears, eyebrows, and chin.

2· Dip the torn newspaper, one piece at a time, into your paper mache mix, and cover all the foil. Let the heads dry.

3· In the back of each head, carefully cut a slit about 3" long that runs up and down, from the top of the head toward the neck. Cut through the paper mache and the foil, but don't break the bulb. Then from the bottom of the bulb, push and twist the light bulb out of the slit. Tape the slit closed. Now add one more layer of paper mache.

4· If you want to have a head that moves, make the neck longer now. Stick your finger into the bottom of the head and wrap foil around the bottom of the head and your finger. Cover the foil with paper mache.

5· When the paper mache is completely dry, paint the head.

TO MAKE THE BODIES

1· Turn the yogurt and cottage cheese containers upside down. When the puppet is finished, your fingers will be the puppet arms. Figure out where you want the center front of the puppet to be. Then cut an armhole on each side of the center for your fingers to fit through. Cut a hole in the top of the container to fit the puppet head in.

2· If your puppet has a head that doesn't move, like the Red Queen, tape the head to the body now.

Why recycle NEWSPAPER ?

Guess what takes up the most space in U.S. landfills (trash dumps). Right—newspapers. By adding water and chemicals, used newspaper gets recycled into pulp to make cereal boxes, egg cartons, construction paper, more newspapers... and many other paper products.

TO MAKE THE RED QUEEN

1· To make the skirt, spread out a brown grocery bag and trace around the bottom of the container. Draw an inner circle about 1" smaller than the first one. Draw an outside circle about 3" to 4" larger than the first one. Cut along the outside and inside circles. This piece is the skirt.

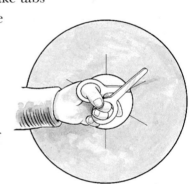

2· To make pleats in the skirt, fold the skirt in half, fold that in half again, fold that in half again until you can't fold anymore. Open it back up. To make tabs to attach the skirt to the body, cut six slits in the waist of the skirt. Make each slit about 1" long and space them evenly around the waist. Tape the tabs to the inside of the body.

3· For the collar, from the grocery bag cut out a circle about 3" across. Draw and cut out a circle about 1" across in the center of the first circle. Cut an opening all the way through the collar. Put the collar around the queen's neck and tape it.

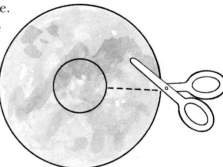

4· Paint the body, the skirt, and the collar.

CᴏᴏL TᴏᴏL

Make Your Own Paper Mache Mix

For some of the projects in this book,
you need to make paper mache.
It's easy...it's kind of gooey or sticky...
so it's fun. Mainly, you tear up old newspaper or brown grocery bags into strips
or little pieces, dip them in
a mix, and stick them on something.
If one kind of paper mache mix works
best for a project, the directions for
that project will say so, but you can use
any of these mixes for any project.

White Glue

In a small bowl or container,
mix 3 parts of white glue and 1 part water.
For instance, 1 cup of glue and
1/3 cup of water.

Wallpaper Paste

Put about a milk gallon jug full of water
in a shallow pan or container—
like a litter box or dishpan.
Sprinkle in about 2 cups
of wallpaper paste mix.
It comes in powder form.
Mix it around with your hands.
It will be lumpy—don't worry.
Add more wallpaper paste mix
or water until the mixture feels
about as thick as runny oatmeal.

Flour

In a small bowl or container,
mix 1 cup of water, 1 cup of flour,
and 1 tablespoon of salt.

TO MAKE THE COUNT

1· For the cape, spread out a brown grocery bag and cut out a square 6" on each side. On one side, mark a point 1½" from each corner. From each of these points, draw a line to the next closest corner. Cut along the lines. Then make a curve in the shortest edge of the cape. This is the neck.

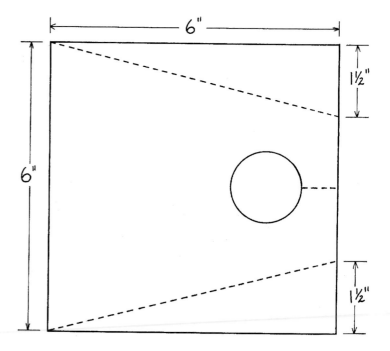

2· Paint the cape and body.

3· Put the puppet head in the top hole of the body. Then attach the cape around the Count's neck with a piece of masking tape underneath. Paint the masking tape to match the cape.

PAPER BAG BOUQUETS

SINCE YOU USE DRIED FLOWERS FOR THESE BOUQUETS, THEY LAST A LONG TIME. IF YOU CAN'T PICK FLOWERS FROM YOUR YARD OR A FRIEND'S GARDEN, YOU CAN FIND DRIED FLOWERS IN A CRAFT DEPARTMENT OR STORE. DRY YOUR OWN FLOWERS BY HANGING THEM UPSIDE DOWN FOR A FEW WEEKS IN A DRY DARK PLACE. SMALL BLOOMS WORK BEST FOR DRYING—AND YOU CAN USE DRIED WEEDS AND GRASSES TOO. INSTEAD OF PAPER BAGS, YOU COULD MAKE SMALL BAGS FROM USED GIFT WRAP, COMIC PAGES, OR CALENDAR PHOTOS.

ECO EXTRA
Nature's Recyclers

Some creatures do nothing but clean up. They're nature's great recyclers, the scavengers. Everything they eat is dead (before you get too disgusted, think about what you eat). For instance, vultures. You've seen them circling high in the sky, riding the air currents, looking for food. They help keep the earth tidy.

WHAT YOU NEED

• Dried flowers
• Small brown paper bags
• Sand, beans, rice, or bird seed for the base
• Scissors or clippers
• Raffia, twine, yarn, ribbon, or string

WHAT TO DO

1· Cut your bag to the size you want. Fill it with sand, beans, rice, or bird seed. This will hold the flower stems and also keep your bag from falling over.

Why recycle PHONE BOOKS?

When new phone books come out every year, most people just throw their old ones in the trash—and you know where the trash goes. Right to the dump. But recycled phone books get turned into ceiling tiles, book covers, and insulation to keep houses warm in winter.

2· Cut the stems of your flowers short enough so they don't fall over when you stick them in the bag.

3· Tie string or raffia around the neck of the bag.

PAPER BAG BOOKS

RECYCLING GROCERY BAGS INTO BOOKS IS A REAL EARTH-SAVER. YOU CAN MAKE THE BOOKS ANY SIZE YOU WANT, WITH AS MANY PAGES AS YOU NEED. USE THEM FOR PHOTO ALBUMS AND DIARIES...FOR WRITING POEMS AND STORIES...AS GIFTS... SKETCH PADS...NATURE JOURNALS. RAID YOUR ART SUPPLIES BOX FOR DECORATIONS (SEE PAGE 135).

WHAT YOU NEED

- Brown paper grocery bags
- Scissors
- White glue, rubber glue, or a glue stick
- Embroidery thread and needle
- An awl
- Decorations—photos, lace, buttons, pebbles, paper, pictures from magazines, wallpaper scraps

WHAT TO DO

1· Cut the bottom off the paper bag. Cut up the side of the bag to make one flat piece. Decide how big you want your book. You can cut this piece in half or in four quarters. Fold the pieces so the writing is on the inside. Glue the insides together to make pages. Use as many bags as you need to make the number of pages you want.

2· Fold the pages in half. Stack the pages, one inside the other. Make holes along the fold with an awl, for your needle to go through.

3· If you're using embroidery thread, use three or four strands. Make a knot at one end of your thread. Sew along the fold, and make a knot at the other end when you're finished.

4· Decorate the cover of your book.

ECO-ENVELOPES

HELP THE EARTH BY MAKING ENVELOPES FROM MAGAZINES AND CALENDARS...AND MAKE SPECIAL ENVELOPES FOR SPECIAL PEOPLE AT THE SAME TIME.

Any fool can destroy trees. They cannot run away.... Through all the wonderful, eventful centuries... God has cared for these trees...but he cannot save them from fools—only Uncle Sam can do that.

—John Muir, *American Forests*

WHAT YOU NEED
- Cardboard or stiff paper
- Magazines, junk mail, catalogues, calendars
- Some envelopes
- A ruler
- Scissors
- White glue, rubber glue, or a glue stick
- Scrap paper

WHAT TO DO

You can make your envelopes any size you want to, but the post office will not deliver mail smaller than 3½" by 5". So be sure any envelope you want to mail is bigger than that.

1· If you want to make standard-sized envelopes, trace different sizes of envelopes on your cardboard. Cut these out.

2· Cut out pictures from old magazines, catalogues, and calendars. Either fold them around the cardboard to make your envelopes, or just fold them to the size you want them.

3· One way to fold them is to fold under about ½" on all four sides. Glue this edge down. Then fold the paper almost in half, but leave about 1" sticking out at the top for your envelope flap. Fold and glue the inside edges.

4· Cut out a label from scrap paper and glue it on.

✳NATURE'S GARDENS BOTTLES AND JARS

HOW SIMPLE IS THIS? RECYCLED JARS AND BOTTLES PLUS PAINT...AND YOU HAVE A NEAT DECORATION...OR A VASE, OR A CANDY JAR, OR A GIFT. ADD GOOD LAMP OIL AND A WICK FROM A CRAFT STORE (SEE THE PHOTO), AND YOU'VE CREATED AN UNUSUAL "CANDLE." (GET ADULT HELP IF YOU WANT TO MAKE A CANDLE.) ASK FRIENDS TO SAVE BOTTLES AND JARS FOR YOU, BECAUSE ONCE YOU GET STARTED, EVERYONE WILL WANT ONE.

WHAT YOU NEED

- Used bottles and jars
- A used plastic lid or old saucer for paint
- Acrylic paints and small paint brushes or paint pens
- Towels or rags
- Lamp oil and candle wicks if you want to make "candles"

WHAT TO DO

1· Wash your bottles and jars in warm soapy water and let them sit in the water awhile to soak the labels off. You may need to scrub them off with a rough cloth or plastic scrubby.

2· Be sure the outside of a jar or bottle is dry before you start painting. Paint on your design with acrylic paint or with paint pens. Paint pens cost more but are very easy to work with.

Paper or Plastic?

You probably knew that paper bags were made out of trees, but did you know that plastic bags are made from oil? And that making either kind of bag pollutes the environment? Think how many bags we all throw away every week!

What can you do about it? When you buy a candy bar or a pack of notebook paper and the clerk starts to put it in a bag, you can say, "I don't need a bag." You might need a bag if you're buying 10 apples, for instance. But when you don't need a bag, don't take one. Just say no.

You can also save bags and reuse them. Try storing them in a reused plastic bottle (page 86). Projects in this book show you how to make hats, bouquets, and books out of paper grocery bags. You can also reuse plastic and paper bags by taking them shopping and using them instead of new bags. Or you can reuse them to carry things, like books you're taking back to the library.

Paper or plastic? What if you answered, "Neither one"? You can, every time you remember to bring your backpack or your own bag with you. You might not want to say to the clerk, "Hey, I care about the earth. I'm protecting the environment." But you could think it.

Recycling Kids, Inc.

How can a baby food jar help save a humpback whale? When you decorate it, fill it with candy, and sell it...then use the money to adopt a whale. That's the kind of project third graders do at Twin Lakes School in El Monte, California.

They run a business called Recycling Kids, Inc. Every year, students in June Burton's class take over the business from last year's students.

- First, they collect trash from school and at home—milk caps, detergent lids, film capsules, tissue boxes, all kinds of throw-aways...
- Then they paint them, or glue on ribbons and decorations and stickers, and turn them into...
- Bird feeders, candle holders, candy jars, pencil boxes, desk sets—50 items altogether—and...

  Sell them on holidays to other students and in the community, so they can...
- Adopt endangered species and endangered habitats.

So far Recycling Kids, Inc., has adopted
five **MANATEES**,
five **HUMPBACK WHALES**,
four acres of **RAINFOREST**,
and two species of **DOLPHINS**.

WANT TO KNOW MORE?
Write to:
Recycling Kids, Inc.
3900 Gilman Road, Room 3
El Monte, CA 91732

TURNING TRASH INTO TREASURES: *Third graders in Recycling Kids, Inc., make magnets and wind chimes from juice lids... Happy Earth pins from milk caps.*

OTALY RECYCLED ALBUMS

ALL REUSED MATERIALS...QUICK AND EASY TO MAKE...PERFECT GIFTS FOR FRIENDS... JUST WHAT YOU NEED FOR THE PHOTOS FROM YOUR VACATION OR THE JOURNAL OF YOUR FIRST CRAZY YEAR IN MIDDLE SCHOOL. (WHO KNEW IT WOULD BE SO MUCH FUN?)

WHAT YOU NEED

- 10 to 12 sheets of recycled office copy paper
- String, scrap cross-current wire, or other fine wire
- Bubble wrap or polyethylene foam wrap (white or green packing material)
- White craft glue
- A needle big enough for your string or wire
- An awl or ice pick
- Scissors
- A flattened out cardboard box to work on

WHAT TO DO

1· Ask someone you know who works in an office for some recycled copy paper. You need paper that has only been used on one side. Cut the pages to the size you want. Cut packing foam or bubble wrap to fit your pages. Cut 2 covers for each book. Stack your pages between the covers.

2· Spread the cardboard on your work surface. Ask an adult to help you make 5 holes on the right-hand edge of your book with the awl or ice pick, ½" from the edge, an equal distance apart.

3· Thread your needle with string or wire. Sew your book together using one of the methods here or one you make up yourself. Then decorate your book as you like. (For photo albums, bubble-wrap and other transparent covers don't really need any decoration—the photos show through.)

Sewing Method #1

1· Push the needle up through the center hole, letting the tail end of the thread hang loose. Sew around the spine and back up through the same hole.

2· Going toward the bottom of the book, sew down into the next 2 holes in the same way. Wrap the thread around the spine as before.

3· Bring your thread around the lower edge of the spine and sew back up through the spine. When you get to the fourth and fifth hole, sew as before. Then sew back down the spine to finish where you began. Tie off your thread tightly.

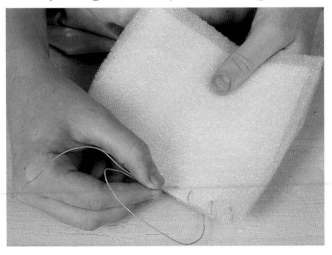

Sewing Method #2

Whipstitch the edge with a single strand of wire. At the top and bottom of the spine, simply wrap the wire off at the end and cut it close to the book.

CALENDAR BOXES

WHAT A GREAT WAY TO SAVE TREES! (EVERY TIME YOU REUSE PAPER, THINK OF IT AS SAVING PART OF A TREE.) DEPENDING ON HOW THICK YOUR CALENDAR PAGES ARE, YOU CAN MAKE TERRIFIC GIFT BOXES, JEWELRY BOXES, OR JUST NEAT-LOOKING BOXES FOR THE FUN OF IT. IT'S REALLY EASY—BET YOU CAN'T MAKE JUST ONE! (YOU DON'T NEED GLUE, BUT TO MAKE THE BOX LAST LONGER, YOU MIGHT WANT TO USE A FEW DABS FROM A GLUE STICK.)

WHAT YOU NEED
- Old calendars or other paper
- Scissors

WHAT TO DO

1· Pick out a calendar picture you like. Fold your picture in half and measure the short side. Then cut the longer side to the same length. Now cut the picture in half, so you have two squares. You will use one square to make the top of your box and one to make the bottom.

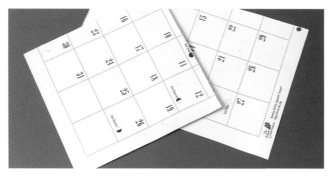

Why recycle ALUMINUM CANS?

Every three months in the United States we throw away enough aluminum to rebuild all the planes in all U.S. airlines. In recycling, aluminum cans get melted, pressed into sheets, and shaped into new cans or other things made of aluminum.

2· Fold one square in half diagonally—matching opposite corners.

3· Open the square. With a corner pointed toward you, fold the right-hand corner into the center of the square.

4· Fold the right-hand side to the center line. Refold these same folds two or three times.

5· Open the square. Do the same folds and refolds on the left-hand side. When you open the square you will have seven fold lines going up and down, evenly spaced.

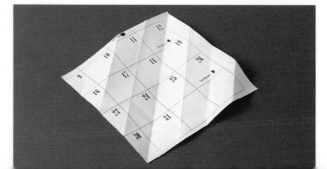

6· Turn the square so the fold lines go across. Fold in half diagonally again and repeat the folds with the new right-hand and left-hand corners.

7· When you open the square you will have fold lines running across and down, forming squares. With one corner pointed toward you, cut along the two lines on either side of the center line, cutting two squares up from the bottom point. Now make these same cuts from the opposite point.

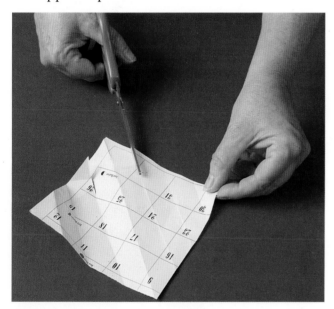

8· Make the sides of the box by folding in the long, uncut corners to the center, then fold in the cut corners—all four points meet in the center.

9· Stand up the four sides of the box.

10· Turn in the points of the long flaps and fold the ends under, then slip the ends under the short (cut) flap on one side, then on the other side. Here's your box bottom. Repeat these steps for the top, and you've made your first box.

Hurray for the Tree Musketeers!

The Earth might not get saved by adults with big ideas. It might get saved by kids starting out with little ones.

In 1987, a Brownie troop in El Segundo, California, used paper plates on a camping trip. They decided to pay the earth back for the plates by planting a sapling—they called it Marcie the Marvelous Tree. They were eight years old.

Some of the Brownies decided they wanted to plant more trees in their community, enough to make a pollution barrier around their town. They called themselves the Tree Musketeers. To get more people interested, they put on TV quiz shows called "Tree Stumpers." Kids ran the cameras, wrote the shows, and produced them. The Tree Musketeers founders were ten years old.

TREE MUSKETEERS *founder Tara Church made a speech to the El Segundo, California, City Council when she was nine. She invited the community to the 1988 Arbor Day celebration.*

The Musketeers Branch Out

When the founders were eleven, Tree Musketeers opened their town's first recycling center. The next year they led the committee that wrote their town's waste management plan. They helped plan a national urban forest conference.

In 1993, Tree Musketeers held the National Youth Environmental Summit, the first national environmental conference organized by kids. The founders were fourteen. When they were sixteen, they held a second conference, the Second National Partners for the Planet Youth Summit—600 young people came from environmental groups all over the country.

Today Marcie the Marvelous Tree is 50 feet tall, and the founders of Tree Musketeers are college age.

- Tree Musketeers has planted more than 700 trees in their hometown.
- The group sends out **Grassroots Youth Magazine** every two months to more than 50,000 readers.
- The Partners for the Planet network supports kids' environmental activities all over the country.

TO START YOUR OWN CLUB
or hook up with Partners for the Planet, write to:
Tree Musketeers
136 Main Street, Dept. P
El Segundo, CA 90245

GROWN UP: *Tara Church at seventeen spoke at the capitol building in Salt Lake City, Utah. Tree Musketeers, founded by a Brownie troop in 1987, was sponsoring a national meeting for kids, called the 1995 Partners for the Planet Youth Summit.*

THAT CAN'T BE PAPER! BEADS

YOU WON'T BELIEVE HOW REALISTIC PAPER BEADS CAN LOOK UNTIL YOU'VE TRIED THIS. THIS MAKES A GREAT ACTIVITY FOR A PARTY, TOO...AND EVERYONE HAS A NECKLACE OR BRACELET TO WEAR HOME. IT'S SO EASY, YOU CAN INVITE LITTLE BROTHERS AND SISTERS TO JOIN IN—YOU CAN CUT THE PAPER UP FOR THEM.

WHAT YOU NEED

- Bright-colored paper from magazines, gift wrap, catalogues, etc.
- White glue or a glue stick
- Scissors
- String, yarn, fishing line, plastic-coated wire, etc.

WHAT TO DO

1. Cut long, skinny triangles of paper, about 1" wide and 4" long.

2. For each bead, smear glue on half of one triangle, toward the tip.

3. As you roll each triangle up, leave a hole through the middle for your string to go through.

4. When the glue has dried, string the beads into necklaces and bracelets.

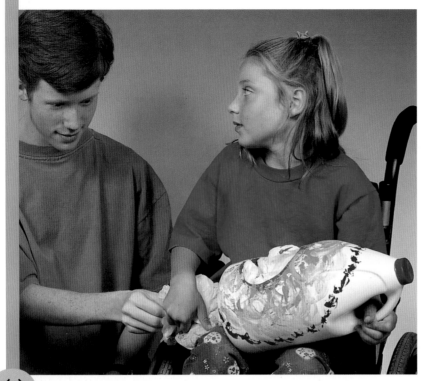

EASY RECYCLE BIN

WHAT YOU NEED
- A large heavy-plastic bottle, washed out with soapy water
- Strong scissors or a knife
- Acrylic paints and a paintbrush

WHAT TO DO

Cut or carve out a hole in the side of the bottle, then paint the bottle in bright colors. Or you can glue on pictures cut from magazines and comic strips...or any other paper.

YOU'LL BE AMAZED AT HOW MANY PLASTIC BAGS YOU CAN STORE IN THIS EASY-TO-MAKE STORAGE BIN. IT'S A GREAT WAY TO RECYCLE PLASTIC BAGS AND TO REUSE PLASTIC BOTTLES. YOU CAN MAKE RECYCLING EVEN EASIER FOR YOUR FAMILY BY GIVING A BIN TO EACH PERSON, DECORATED JUST FOR THEM.

Why recycle PLASTIC?

Every hour, people in the United States throw out 2.5 million plastic bottles and jugs—that's enough to wrap around the earth 4 times in a year. Picture that for a minute. Recycled plastic milk jugs and soda bottles get shredded, melted, and made into vests, carpet, t-shirts, and teddy bears.

Is That a SODA BOTTLE You're Wearing?

Okay, so what happens to all those newspapers and plastic bottles and glass and cans you put in the recycle bins?

Imagine pajamas and t-shirts made out of soda bottles...bikes made from old refrigerators and milk jugs...sandals with soles made of tires. Sound like science fiction? Nope. It's here and it's now and it's good for the planet.

Sometimes, the stuff you recycle gets turned back into what it was—that's what happens to most glass, aluminum cans, and paper.

But...used plastic bottles get shredded and melted and turned into...carpets... t-shirts...hats, gloves, and jackets. Your new bike or wagon might have steel parts made from steel cans, old cars, and appliances like washing machines. The soles of those sandals in your closet might once have been tires.

Only certain companies make things from recycled materials. This is a good reason to read labels and tags before you buy something. If you see the recycling symbol on a label, either the product itself or the package is made of recycled materials. Sometimes instead the package will say "Made of recycled materials."

You be the recycling detective—check out paper towels, baseball bats, cans, skateboards, writing paper, greeting cards, cereal boxes. Whenever you choose something recycled instead of something made of all new materials, you're helping the planet stay healthy.

RECYCLED FASHION SHOW: *Students at Erwin High School in Asheville, North Carolina, gave a fashion show to promote recycling at a Career Expo Day. These cherry-red long johns are made of recycled plastic soda bottles and reclaimed cotton. The teddy bear fabric comes entirely from plastic soda bottles, and the wagon wheels and steel are from recycled materials.*

RE(BI)CYCLED? *Sports equipment like this bike and golf club can be made from recycled materials—steel from old cars and appliances, plastic parts from milk jugs, grips and pedals from recycled rubber... and a bike pack from plastic soda bottles.*

PICTURE-PERFECT POSTCARDS

WHAT MAKES THESE POSTCARDS PERFECT IS THAT YOU TAKE THE PICTURES, OR CHOOSE THEM, AND YOU MAKE THE POSTCARDS. SEND A POSTCARD OF YOUR DOG TO YOUR COUSIN WHO THINKS HER DOG IS SO GREAT...A POSTCARD OF A COLORFUL AUTUMN TREE TO YOUR FRIEND IN MIAMI WHO NEVER GETS TO SEE FALL COLORS... A POSTCARD OF YOURSELF TO EVERYONE!

WHAT YOU NEED

- Light-colored, thin cardboard from old boxes (cereal boxes, for instance). You can also use poster board.
- Scissors
- A ruler
- White glue, rubber glue, or a glue stick
- Photographs or pictures from magazines

WHAT TO DO

1· If you're using photographs, trace around your photograph onto the cardboard. If you're using other pictures, draw a rectangle on the cardboard about 6" by 4". Cut it out.

2· On the side you will write on (the blank side on cereal-box cardboard), draw a line across the card to divide it for the message and the address. Glue your photo or pictures on the other side. Be sure to glue it on tight. If it comes off, your friends will wonder why you're writing to them on a cereal box.

Why recycle
CORRUGATED CARDBOARD?

Making new corrugated boxes out of recycled cardboard uses up much less energy and creates much less pollution than making them from trees. Brown paper bags are made of the same paper as cardboard— you can find out from your recycler if you can recycle them with corrugated cardboard.

COOL CUT-AND-PASTE BOTTLES AND JARS

A S EASY AS CUTTING AND PASTING...AND A PLANET-SAVING WAY TO REUSE GLASS OR PLASTIC. THE FANCY NAME FOR THIS CUT-AND-PASTE METHOD IS DECOUPAGE. YOU CAN DECOUPAGE JUST ABOUT ANYTHING—FURNITURE, BOXES, TRAYS, YOUR LITTLE BROTHER.

WHAT YOU NEED
- Used bottles and jars
- Vases from garage sales or secondhand stores
- Old magazines, photos, drawings, fabric scraps
- Decoupage glue from a craft department
- A glue brush
- Sandpaper
- For the Ocean of Fish bottle: sand and food color

WHAT TO DO

1· Wash your bottles and jars in warm soapy water. Let them sit in the water to soak the labels off. You may need to scrub them off with a rough cloth or plastic scrubby.

2· Look at magazine pictures, junk mail, old clothes, wallpaper samples, ticket stubs, play programs, or any paper or fabric at all to choose what you want to glue on your bottle.

3· Brush decoupage glue on a piece of your paper or fabric and stick it on your bottle or jar. You might want to glue on just a few things...

4· Or you might want to cover your whole bottle.

5· After you've glued everything on, brush a coat of decoupage glue over the whole design. Let the glue dry. You can add more coats of glue to seal your design better.

6· You can sand between each coat or sand after all your coats of glue. See which effect you like. You can use a clean rag to wipe off the sanded glue so your bottle is smooth.

TO MAKE AN OCEAN OF FISH BOTTLE

1· Glue on fish from fabric or pictures of fish. Brush layers of glue over them and sand them smooth.

2· Put some sand in the bottom of your bottle or jar.

3· Pour in water and add a little blue or green food color.

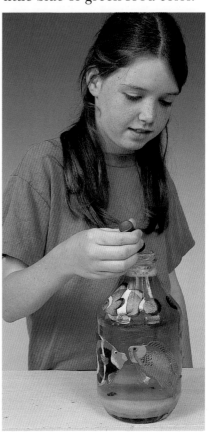

Why recycle GLASS?

Making glass out of recycled materials cuts air pollution by up to 20 percent. Used glass bottles and jars are recycled by crushing and melting them, then making them into new glass products.

4 Terrific Eco-TRASH

FANTASTIC FLOWER POTS

EVERY GARDENER HAS STACKS OF MUDDY, MOSS-COVERED TERRA-COTTA (CLAY) FLOWERPOTS LYING AROUND THAT YOU CAN TURN INTO TRULY TERRIFIC POTS WITH JUST A LITTLE PAINT...AND A LOT OF FUN. HAVE A POT-PAINTING PARTY! YOU CAN FILL YOUR WINDOWSILLS WITH THESE POTS, AND PEOPLE ALSO LOVE TO GET THEM AS GIFTS.

WHAT YOU NEED

- A terra cotta pot and saucer, scrubbed clean with water and dried. If you can't find a terra cotta saucer, use any saucer or plastic lid.
- Acrylic paints
- Small paintbrushes
- Urethane sealer
- A larger paintbrush for the urethane
- Paint thinner for cleaning the brush
- Rags
- A jar of water

93

WHAT TO DO

1· To prepare your pot and saucer, paint them with a very thin coat of urethane sealer. This is so your paint will stay on the surface of the pot, instead of being absorbed by the clay. Clean your brush with paint thinner and a rag. Let the pot and saucer dry completely. This takes at least 12 hours.

2· Decide on your design. If you want to, you can draw your design in pencil before you paint. After you paint on one color, let that color dry. Swish your brush in the water to clean it, and wipe it with a rag before you go on to the next color.

3· When all the paint is dry, seal the pot and saucer with another thin coat of urethane. Keep brushing the urethane on lightly, and try not to let it drip or run down the side of the pot. Clean your brush with paint thinner and a rag, and wait at least 12 hours for your pot and saucer to dry...then add potting soil and a plant!

DOG BISCUIT PHOTO FRAME

WHAT YOU NEED
- Old picture frame
- Dog biscuits
- Gold paint (or any color you like)
- Craft glue

WHAT TO DO

1. Glue the dog biscuits to the frame. (Or you might think it's easier to paint the frame first, let it dry, then glue on the biscuits, then paint the biscuits.)

RECYCLE AN OLD PICTURE FRAME INTO THE PERFECT FRAME FOR YOUR DOG'S PICTURE. OR GIVE THIS FUNNY FRAME TO A FRIEND WHO LOVES THEIR DOG.

2. Paint the biscuits and the frame.

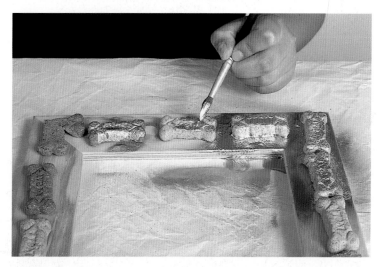

95

EGGSHELL MOSAIC

WHAT YOU NEED

- Eggshells
- Food coloring
- Water
- Small paintbrushes
- A piece of corrugated cardboard
- White glue
- A pencil
- 4 or 5 cups or bowls (1 for each color)
- Vinegar
- Newspaper

THE HARDEST THING ABOUT MAKING THESE PICTURES IS WAITING UNTIL YOU HAVE SAVED UP ENOUGH EGGSHELLS. YOU NEED SHELLS FROM ABOUT 12 EGGS—JUST RINSE THEM AND STORE THEM IN THE REFRIGERATOR UNTIL YOU'RE READY TO USE THEM. THE MOSAIC IN THE PHOTO SHOWS HOT-AIR BALLOONS RISING OVER MOUNTAINS.

WHAT TO DO

You can color your eggshells ahead of time, or you can paint them after you glue them on the cardboard, or you can do some shells each way.

1· If you're coloring your eggshells before you glue them, mix one color of food coloring in each cup or bowl to the shade you want. Add a teaspoon of vinegar to each color. Then put some eggshells in each color and leave them there overnight. In the morning, lay them on newspaper to dry.

2· Sketch your design on the cardboard, if you want to. Then spread glue on the cardboard and glue on the eggshells according to your design. You can break the shells into smaller pieces to fit them to the space, if you need to.

3· If you glue on white eggshells, paint them with a brush to make your design. You can add trims of beads, ribbon, string, or other items for decoration. You can also glue a frame on your picture made from ribbon, rope, or whatever you like.

Mosaic—An Earth-Friendly Art

Most artists care very deeply about saving the earth and its beauty. Mosaic artists often re-use materials like colored glass and tile to make their beautiful pictures and designs. They also use natural materials like stones and pebbles. Terry Taylor made this bird feeder and garden stepping stone from broken plates.

Artists have made mosaics for more than 2,000 years—at least. Buildings all around the world have whole ceilings, walls, and floors decorated with mosaics hundreds of years old. Near Mexico City, mosaics cover the outside of an entire 10-story library built not long ago. Today people have mosaics on their garden walls, patios, and walks. Or hanging on their walls, like this dog mosaic by George Fishman.

Keep your eyes open— you can probably spot mosaics in the town where you live.

LICENSE PLATE BIRD FEEDER

WHAT YOU NEED

- 2 license plates
- 4 thick sticks for the uprights, 5½" long
- 4 thick sticks for floor sides, 2 about 12" long and 2 about 8½" long
- Plywood scrap for floor, about 8½" by 9¼"
- Wood scraps for roof ends, to make 2 triangles about 10½" long by 3" at the point
- 8 #10 tapping screws, 5/8" long
- 8 #6 galvanized dry-wall screws, 1 5/8" long
- 10 #6 galvanized dry-wall screws, 1¼" long
- A screwdriver
- A handsaw
- A pencil
- A ruler
- A hammer and a nail
- Twine or wire

WHAT TO DO

1· With your ruler and a pencil, on your wood scraps measure 2 triangles for the roof ends. The base should be about 10½". Then measure 3" up from the middle of the base, and draw lines from that point to each end of the base to make a triangle. On the plywood scrap, measure a rectangle for your floor, about 8½" by 10¼". Unless you have had a lot of practice with a handsaw, ask an adult to help you saw these pieces out.

EXCEPT FOR THE SCREWS, THIS BIRD FEEDER IS ENTIRELY RECYCLED—FROM OLD LICENSE PLATES, WOOD SCRAPS, AND BRANCHES FROM FALLEN TREES. BE SURE TO HANG IT NEAR SOME BUSHES OR TREES, SO THE BIRDS HAVE A SAFE PLACE TO FLY TO NEARBY. YOUR BIRD VISITORS WILL LIKE YOUR RESTAURANT EVEN BETTER IF YOU OFFER THEM SOME WATER ALONG WITH THE BIRDSEED. YOU CAN RECYCLE AN ALUMINUM PAN FROM A FROZEN DINNER FOR A BIRDBATH...OR USE A LARGE TERRA COTTA SAUCER FROM A FLOWERPOT.

2. Make a few holes in the floor piece so rain water can drain out of your feeder. You can make these with a hammer and nail or with screws and the screwdriver.

3. Saw the 4 sticks that fit around your floor to the right lengths. Screw these to the edges of the floor with the 1¼" dry-wall screws. First screw in the 2 sticks that fit along the short sides of the floor. Then attach the long sticks. They will stick out about an inch on each end.

4. Saw the 4 sticks to hold up your roof—called uprights—to the same length. Screw 2 uprights to each roof end, using 4 dry-wall screws 1⅝" long. Follow the picture.

5. Holding a roof end parallel to the short side of the floor, screw the bottom of the uprights to the corners of the floor, using 1 dry-wall screw 1⅝" long for each upright. A helper comes in handy for this step.

6. Screw the license plates to the roof ends to finish your roof, using the tapping screws. Run twine or wire through the roof to hang your feeder.

You're Invited!

To What?
A WILDLIFE PARTY
Where?
YOUR BACKYARD, DECK, OR PATIO
When?
AS SOON AS YOU CAN GET ORGANIZED

You don't have any wild animals in your yard? What about those squirrels on your patio? And those ferocious butterflies? And that man-eating chickadee?

You probably have some other wild animals around that you don't even know about. If you keep a bird feeder full of seed, you can be pretty sure that flying squirrels visit it at night. Chipmunks and raccoons like to party around houses. So do mice. Toads. Moles. Rabbits. Possums. Bats. When you think about it, your backyard looks a lot like a jungle. It's pretty wild out there already!

If you want to help protect some of these wild creatures, you and your family can:

• *Offer them a drink. Water will bring you more wild guests than anything else you can offer. Make a backyard wetland (page 39). Or a birdbath. Butterflies need damp earth to drink from—they can't drink from a birdbath.*

• *Plant trees and bushes for food and shelter. Ask your local garden center what will be best.*

• *Plant bright flowers for butterflies.*

• *Plant sweet-smelling white flowers for moths and bats.*

• *Plant red flowers for hummingbirds or put up a hummingbird feeder.*

• *Start a pile of branches for small animals to hide in.*

• *Hang bird feeders in safe places, and keep them filled with mixed birdseed and sunflower seed.*

• *Put up birdhouses. Find out from a bird book what kinds are best and how to hang them.*

• *If you have a cat, put a bell on its collar to warn birds and small animals.*

CORNY SUNFLOWERS

N0 ONE WILL GUESS WHAT YOUR SUNFLOWERS ARE MADE OF! YOU CAN DRY YOUR OWN CORNHUSKS FOR THIS PROJECT. SEE PAGE 103.

WHAT YOU NEED

- Dried cornhusks. If you never eat corn on the cob, you can get these at a craft store.
- A seed pod or small pinecone for the center. Or you can make a center out of cornhusk, or draw one and color it brown.
- Sticks, wire, coat hanger, chopstick, pick-up stick, or pipe cleaner for stems
- White craft glue, or a low-temperature glue gun with glue
- Yellow and green markers or food coloring or cloth dye
- Scissors

WHAT TO DO

1· Color the cornhusks. You can dye them in food coloring mixed with water or in cloth dye—you can get both from the grocery store. Just follow the directions. Or you can color the husks with yellow and green markers. When the husks are dry, cut out petals and leaves. The flowers in the picture each have about 18 or 20 petals and 2 leaves.

2· Glue the stem to the sunflower center with white glue or a glue gun. If it's a sharp stick, stick it through the center, then glue it. One petal at a time, glue half the petals to the center, making a complete circle of petals. If you use a glue gun, ask an adult for help.

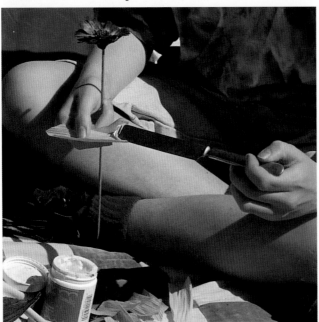

3· If you use white glue, let the first layer of petals dry before you start the second layer. Glue more petals under the first layer, making another complete circle of petals. These petals should show in between the petals of the first layer. If you have petals left, after your glue has dried, add a third layer of petals.

4· Glue the leaves under the petals.

COOL TOOL

Dry Your Own CORNHUSKS

Native American Indians used cornhusks to weave clothing or wrap food for cooking. Tamales, a Mexican food, are made by mixing ground meat and seasonings, rolling the mixture in cornmeal dough, and wrapping the little pies in cornhusks to steam them. To eat a tamale, you unwrap the cornhusks, like opening a package.

Besides the angels and sunflowers in this book, you'll probably discover lots of other cornhusk projects you would like to make. So it's a good idea to know how to dry your own husks. It's easy, it's cheap, and you get to eat the corn on the cob.

All you do is this:

- Save the husks after you peel them off the corn and let them dry in the air for two or three days— in the sun, if you can.

- You could lay them out on newspaper to dry or hang them on a line with clothespins. If you put them on newspaper, turn them over every day so they don't mildew.

- Then store them in a box until you're ready to use them.

You can leave husks their natural color, like the angels in this book, or you can paint or dye them, like the sunflowers.

TOO STIFF? To make dry cornhusks easier to work with, soak them in hot water for a few minutes right before you use them. Then lay them on a towel, ready to be turned into angels, sunflowers, dolls, baskets, hats, or whatever you dream up.

CORNHUSK ANGELS

ANGELS ARE HANDY TO HAVE AROUND ANY TIME, NOT JUST AT CHRISTMAS. MAYBE SOMEONE YOU KNOW NEEDS A GUARDIAN ANGEL RIGHT NOW. YOU CAN DRY YOUR OWN CORNHUSKS FOR THESE ANGELS OR GET THEM AT A CRAFT STORE. (TO DRY YOUR OWN, SEE PAGE 103.)

WHAT YOU NEED (FOR ONE ANGEL)

- About 8 dried cornhusks
- For the head, a little clay, play dough, or putty (anything you can stick wire through)
- Some thin wire, string, or raffia
- A 3" piece of heavy wire
- Scissors
- White glue or craft glue
- Bits of cloth, lace, and ribbon, tinsel or aluminum foil scraps
- Corn silk or yarn for hair, if you want it

WHAT TO DO

Soak the cornhusks in hot water for about fifteen minutes to soften them.

TO MAKE THE HEAD

1· For the head, make a ball of clay about as big as an acorn.

2· Make a fishhook in one end of your heavy wire. Now make a piece of husk about 2½" wide and 5" long. Pinch it in the middle and put the wire hook around the pinched middle.

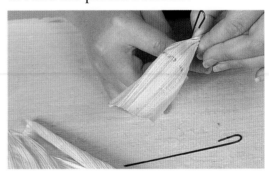

3· Stick the other end of the wire into the top of the clay head and push it all the way through until just the end of the hook with the cornhusk in it shows at the top.

4· To finish the head, wrap the two ends of the husk over the ball to cover it. Twist a piece of thin wire (or string or raffia) around the neck to hold the husk tight. Cut the ends of the wire short.

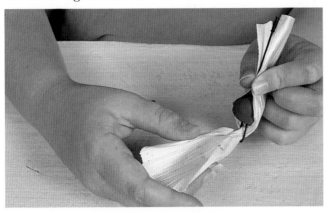

TO MAKE THE BODY AND ROBE

1· Spread out a bigger piece of husk, about 8" or 9" long. Lay the head in one end of the husk and tie the end around the neck with another piece of thin wire, string, or raffia.

2· Now pull the long end of the husk over the wire and the short end so they don't show.

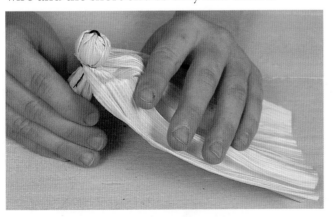

TO MAKE THE WINGS

1· For each wing, you need a strip of husk about 8" long. Hold the ends together.

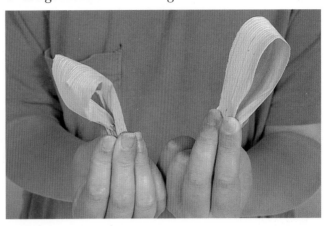

2· Having a helper for this step makes it easier. Hold the ends of the wings at the back of the angel's waist. Tie string, raffia, or thin wire around the waist and the wings to hold them on. You might want to wrap it around a few times.

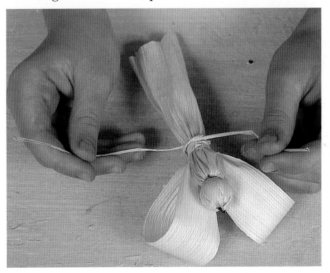

TO FINISH YOUR ANGEL

Decorate your angel any way you want to—it's your angel. You could make a sash out of any fabric or ribbon and tie it on. You might glue on hair made from corn silk or yarn. For a halo, you can make a loop of gold or silver ribbon, tinsel, or aluminum foil and glue it on.

BEACH GLASS JEWELRY

WHEN BOTTLES END UP IN THE OCEAN, THEY BREAK INTO SMALL PIECES. STIRRED AROUND AND AROUND BY THE WAVES AND SAND, THE PIECES OF GLASS END UP ON THE BEACH, SMOOTH AS BEACH PEBBLES. YOU'LL HAVE AS MUCH FUN COLLECTING BEACH GLASS AS YOU WILL MAKING GREAT PENDANTS, PINS, OR EARRINGS WITH IT. BETTER COME HOME WITH PLENTY OF EXTRA GLASS TO MAKE JEWELRY FOR FRIENDS!

WHAT YOU NEED

- Beach glass
- Jewelry bails (tiny clamps)
- Pin and earring backs
- Cord (whatever you like)
- Jewelry cement or silicon glue
- Scissors

WHAT TO DO

1. Pick out pieces of glass you like. Use the flattest pieces for pins. Any shape works for pendants or earrings.

2. To make a pin or pendant, glue two or three pieces together if you want to. When the glue is dry, glue a pin-back on the pin and allow to dry. For a pendant, glue a jewelry bail to one edge. Leave enough space at the top to thread your cord through.

3. To make earrings, glue a jewelry bail to one edge of each piece of glass you've chosen. They don't have to match, of course. (Remember not to make the earrings too heavy, unless you want your earlobes dangling around your ankles.) Attach whatever kind of earring fastener you want—you can get them in craft departments.

You Don't Need a Garage for a Garage Sale

Have your own garage sale!

The miracle about garage sales is, other people want stuff you don't want anymore, and they actually pay you for it! Everyone wins. You're helping the planet because other people will reuse your things...they can buy things they want at good prices...and you're making money.

You can hold your sale in your yard, your carport, your driveway...or on the sidewalk...or actually in your garage.

- Figure out what you and your family want to sell. If you don't have enough for a good sale, ask friends or neighbors to join you.

- Gather everything you're going to sell and put price tags on everything.

- Put up posters and notices to advertise the day and time of your sale. Put an ad in the paper about it. Leave yourself plenty of time before the sale begins to put your stuff out.

- On the day of your sale, put your items out so people can see them easily and so they look good. Smile...here comes your first customer!

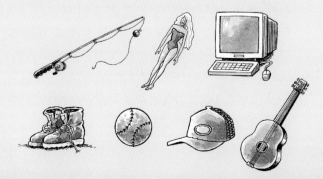

Garage sale today!
Books 50¢
Games 75¢
good soccer stuff
25¢-$2

KISSY FISH PIÑATA

WHAT YOU NEED

- A 12" balloon
- Some newspaper
- Brown paper bags or a big piece of plain newsprint
- Paper mache mix (see page 70). White glue paper mache mix works well for the piñata.
- A bowl
- A 2" square of cardboard
- Masking tape
- 2 paper plates (recycled are fine)
- A sharp knife
- Scissors
- Poster paints and brushes
- Strong string for hanging

PIÑATAS FILLED WITH CANDIES, SMALL GIFTS, AND FRUIT ARE A TRADITION AT BIRTHDAYS AND CHRISTMAS IN LATIN AMERICA. KIDS TAKE TURNS TRYING TO BREAK THE PIÑATA WITH A LONG STICK. SOUNDS EASY—UNTIL YOU FIND OUT THE PERSON WITH THE STICK IS BLINDFOLDED. YOU CAN MAKE PIÑATAS ANY SHAPE YOU WANT. THIS PAPER MACHE KISSING FISH IS MADE MOSTLY FROM NEWSPAPER—BUT DON'T FORGET THE CANDY! (IF YOU DON'T WANT ANYONE TO BREAK YOUR PIÑATA, YOU CAN JUST HANG IT UP FOR DECORATION AND GIVE YOUR GUESTS THE CANDY.)

WHAT TO DO

1· Mix about a pint of paper mache mix in a bowl. Blow up the balloon. Tear a pile of newspaper strips about 5" long and 2" wide. Dip the newspaper strips into the paper mache mix—get them good and wet. Run the strips in different directions, and cover the whole balloon with strips.

2· Brush off the extra mix with a clean brush. Set the balloon in a bowl to drip dry. When that layer is dry, put on another layer of strips. (You can make the layers dry faster by putting the balloon in front of a fan.)

3· When the second layer is dry, with a sharp knife cut a door 3" square in one side of the balloon. Only cut three sides of the door. The balloon will break, but that is okay. Pull the balloon out through the door.

4· Reach through the door to the other side of the piñata and make a small hole for your string to go through. Tie a fat knot on one end of your string. Pull the string through a hole in the 2" square of cardboard. Stick the unknotted end of the string through the door in the piñata, then out the hole on the other side.

5· Fill the piñata with wrapped candies and any other small gifts you want to. Then tape the door shut with masking tape.

6· Cut fins, eyelids, and tail from the edges of paper plates. Make lips from rolled pieces of newspaper taped with masking tape. Tape all these parts to the body with masking tape.

7· Add one more layer of paper mache. Use brown paper bags or plain newsprint if you can, because printed newspaper will show through the paint. Cover all the fish except the fins and eyelids.

8· Paint the fish with poster paints. Let one color dry before you put on the next color.

You're ready for...the party!

109

Trees, Please

Planting a tree is one of the best things you can do to save the Earth.

Right now, for every tree we plant, 30 are getting cut down or burned down.
We have a lot of work to do. Luckily, growing trees is fun.

Don't Plant Palm Trees in Alaska

If you decide to plant a tree, you can buy a young tree from a nursery or you can start with a seed. Even though trees—like us—grow by themselves, you will be like a parent to this tree. You can make sure your tree will be healthy by thinking about a few things before you plant it.

- *What kinds of trees grow well where you live? You can be pretty sure a lemon tree won't grow outdoors in Michigan, and you'll probably be disappointed if you plant a blue spruce in Florida.*

- *Will your tree have plenty of room to grow... up and out? To be sure, find out how tall and how wide your tree will be when it's full grown.*

- *Who will take care of the tree? Just like any other baby, it will need water, food, and love. In the first year, for instance, it needs water every week.*

- *Is the soil okay—will your tree get enough to eat? Will it get enough sun?*

If you think you can make a good home for a tree, you can buy a young tree, called a sapling, from a nursery, or you can plant a seed.

THE MIRACLE OF TREES *begins with seeds. These are honey locust, Douglas fir, and pond pine seeds from Trees for Life. More than 700,000 kids in the United States have planted their own trees through Trees for Life projects.*

DIG IT! *To plant a seedling tree, you start with a hole as deep and twice as wide as your pot.*

Planting a Sapling

Ask at the nursery for any special instructions for planting and caring for your new sapling. Here's what to do for most trees:

- *Dig a hole as high as the pot your sapling is in and two times as wide.*

- *Make sure the soil around your hole is loose, and get rid of any rocks you find.*

- *Take the pot off. If the roots are growing around and around, straighten them out or cut them. If a lot of roots are sticking out of the soil, cut the root ball vertically with your shovel three or four times.*

- *Put the tree in the hole. Make sure when you fill in the hole that the soil comes to the same height on the tree as the soil in the pot did. Pack the soil down by stamping on it to make sure no air pockets are left.*

- *Make a dam around the hole with soil to hold in the water. Water the tree well.*

MULCH IT! *Volunteers spread mulch around a new tree along a highway in North Carolina. Mulch keeps weeds out and water in. You can mulch your new tree with 4" to 6" of wood chips, pine needles, straw, sawdust, or tea grounds. Just don't let the mulch touch the trunk—the bark might rot from not getting enough air.*

Taking Care of Your New Tree

If your tree can't stand up by itself, you need to hold it up with stakes. (Not steaks that you eat, of course.) You can get stakes at a garden center. Tie the tree loosely to the stakes with strips of cloth or other soft material.

For the first year, water your tree with two to three gallons of water every week. Then water it every other week in the summer and once a month in winter.

Rock-a-Bye, Baby

You can plant tree seeds in small pots or half an old milk carton filled with potting soil from a garden center. A few kinds of seeds are ready to grow right away, like Douglas fir and Ponderosa pine. Other seeds that are easy to grow are loblolly pine, bald cypress, date palm, and cabbage palm.

Some seeds need to be prepared first, like honey locust seeds. They must soak in hot water for several days. In fact, most tree seeds are so hard to grow that it's easier to get a sapling from a nursery. Find out if your seeds need special preparation before you plant them. A good place to find out about growing trees from seeds is: Trees for Life, 1103 Jefferson, Wichita, Kansas 67203.

Besides Trees for Life, other groups especially interested in trees are the National Arbor Day Foundation, Trees Corps, and Tree Musketeers. You can find out more about these groups at the library and on the Internet. The U.S. Forest Service also has excellent information on trees.

TREES FOR LIFE: *These kids are transplanting their Trees for Life seedlings from cartons to outdoor homes. Trees for Life started with an eighth-grade class at Wilbur Junior High School in Wichita, Kansas. They held a car wash and earned enough money to plant 103 fruit trees in India. Now Trees for Life has planted more than 30 million fruit trees in many countries...to protect the environment and feed hungry people. One fruit tree can provide more than 10,000 pounds of fruit!*

GOURD WITCH

BESIDES WITCHES, YOU CAN PAINT ALL KINDS OF FACES ON GOURDS. ANIMAL FACES LIKE PIGS AND SHARKS AND RACCOONS...CARTOON FACES...DRACULA OR BATMAN OR EVEN SOMEONE YOU KNOW. FOR WITCH HAIR, INSTEAD OF SPANISH MOSS YOU CAN USE SCRAPS OF YARN OR FABRIC, WEEDS OR STRAW...OR PACKING MATERIAL...OR YOU CAN PAINT HAIR. YOU MIGHT WANT TO PAINT A MUCH SCARIER WITCH THAN THE FRIENDLY ONE IN THIS PICTURE.

WHAT YOU NEED

- A gourd, scrubbed clean with a stiff brush
- A sponge
- A black felt-tip marker
- A pencil
- White glue or paste
- Acrylic paints (for this witch—orange, red, black, and white)
- Small paintbrushes
- An old saucer or plastic lid for paint
- Spanish moss or other pretend hair
- String

WHAT TO DO

1· Tie a string around the stem so you can hang the gourd up to dry. With your marker, draw a line around the top part of the gourd for the hat. Paint the hat black. Hang the gourd to dry.

2· Squeeze or pour some orange paint into your saucer. Dip in your sponge and pat orange paint all over the gourd, except the hat. Hang it to dry. If you need to, sponge on a second coat of orange paint.

3· When the orange paint is completely dry, draw the eyes, nose, and mouth with a pencil. Paint in the white oval eyes and the red nose. Let the paint dry. With your black marker, outline the eyes and nose and draw over the mouth. Draw in the round eye pupil with your pencil, then ink it in with your pen. Dab in the white eye highlights with either end of your paint brush.

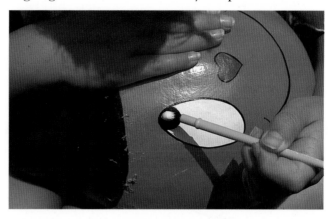

4· Draw a line of thick white glue around the bottom of the hat. Press on Spanish moss or some other hair.

ECO EXTRA

The oldest living things on earth are trees.

The oldest tree is 4,600 years old. It is a bristlecone pine in California.

Eco-Party

The next time you have a party,
you can make it a special celebration
of the Earth too. Lots of the
Earth-friendly projects in this book
are perfect for parties...
maybe you've thought of that already.

What You Can Make

- Party invitations and envelopes (page 75). On the back of each invitation, you can write, "Made of 100% reused materials."

- Gifts! Everyone loves to get handmade gifts, and this book is full of ideas for them.

- Gift wrap and gift boxes...Wrap presents and prizes in gift wrap you print yourself (page 27)...or in the Sunday comics...or in wrapping paper and ribbon saved from other gifts. Put small gifts in pretty boxes you've made from calendars (page 81).

- A tablecloth or place mats...You can print these yourself too, just like the gift wrap.

- A kissy fish piñata (page 108) full of wrapped candy and little gifts...or just for decoration.

- Sand candles and cornhusk sunflowers for decoration (page 59 and 101)

- Grocery bag party hats (page 30). You can make these ahead of time for your guests, and let them decorate them however they want to at the party.

What Else You Can Do

Use reusable cups and plates instead of paper plates. Usually after paper plates are used, they can't be recycled. If you can't use breakable dishes, use reusable plastic ones.

If you use plastic forks and spoons, wash and save them instead of throwing them away.

Make a special Party Box to store gift wrap and other supplies for your next party!

5. Happenin' Eco-Hits

ROCK HOUSES

WANT TO BE A HOUSEPAINTER? AND HAVE LOADS OF FUN?
ONCE YOU'VE PAINTED ONE OF THESE LITTLE ROCK
HOUSES, YOU'LL PROBABLY WANT TO CREATE A WHOLE
TOWN. THIS IS ALSO GREAT FUN TO DO WITH
FRIENDS...BUILD A CITY...A METROPOLIS...A KINGDOM!

WHAT YOU NEED

- Rocks that look like houses
- A cleaning brush
- A pencil
- Acrylic paints
- Small paintbrushes
- Felt-tip markers

WHAT TO DO

1. Collect rocks that look like houses to you. The bottom of the house needs to be fairly flat, so the house will stand up. Rocks with smooth sides are easier to paint than rough rocks. Scrub your rocks clean with a stiff brush.

2· Look at the rock for awhile, so it can tell you what kind of house it should be. You can also look at pictures of different kinds of houses for ideas. Draw in the general design with a pencil. Draw in the windows, door, roofline, chimney, and other features with a felt-tip pen.

3· Think about colors. Use smaller brushes for little details like shutters. Do one color at a time, and let the paint dry before you do the next color. Try some shading, if you want to—use a little darker shade of a color to show depth. For the tiniest details like shingles or bricks, use a felt-tip pen. If the house has bushes or vines, add them last. Use your pen to draw vines.

PAPER MACHE BIRD

YOU MIGHT WANT TO MODEL SOME OF THE BIRDS YOU SEE NEAR YOUR HOUSE, OR YOU MIGHT RATHER HAVE SOMETHING MORE UNUSUAL SITTING ON A SHELF IN YOUR ROOM, LIKE A PENGUIN OR A YELLOW-BELLIED SAPSUCKER. YOU CAN FIND HUNDREDS OF BIRD PICTURES AT THE LIBRARY AND IN NATURE MAGAZINES, AND MAKE A WHOLE TREE FULL OF BIRDS.

- A picture of a bird
- Wire that you can bend
- Used aluminum foil
- Paper mache mix in a small bowl or pan (see page 70)
- Newspaper
- White latex paint or gesso from a craft store
- Acrylic paints
- Small paintbrushes
- Twig, basket, napkin ring, or other mount

WHAT TO DO

1· Shape your bird from wire—don't forget the feet! Then cover all but the feet with aluminum foil, and shape the bird's body, head, and beak more exactly.

2· Tear newspaper into strips about ¼" wide. Dip them in the paper mache mix and crisscross them all over your bird, except the feet, until the bird is covered. Allow the bird to dry completely. You can dry it faster in front of a fan, or with a hair dryer, or in an oven set at 150 degrees. If you use an oven, ask an adult for help.

3· Paint the whole bird with white latex paint or gesso. Allow it to dry.

4· Paint the bird with acrylic paints, matching the colors in your picture. Once it has dried, you can display your bird on a branch…in a small basket of pebbles or marbles…on a napkin ring…in a little nest of sticks…or whatever you can imagine.

ECO EXTRA

Birds have between 940 and 25,000 feathers, depending on the kind of bird.

A Wonderful Wild Man: JOHN MUIR

More than a hundred years ago, before anyone had ever heard of the word *ecology*, John Muir saw it, believed in it, and wrote about it. He believed every tree and pebble and person and mountain was connected to everything else, all part of the web of life.

> *"When I was a boy in Scotland, I was fond of everything that was wild, and all my life I've been growing fonder and fonder of wild places and wild creatures."*

—John Muir, *The Story of My Boyhood and Youth*

So what's so great about that? Lots of people believe that. But back when John Muir was young, most people *didn't* believe that. Back then the United States was busy wrecking the environment, cutting down all the trees, and stripping coal off the mountains. No land was protected. There were no national parks, no national monuments, and no national forests.

John Muir wrote about the beauty of the mountains and glaciers, and about how precious every creature was. He convinced presidents and Congress of his ideas, and by the time he died, people in the United States had begun to think differently. The government decided that it was important to take care of the land and all the country's natural resources…to use them wisely…to conserve them, to save them for everyone's children and their grandchildren.

IN DUNBAR, SCOTLAND, *the house where John Muir was born is now a memorial museum. Nearby lies John Muir Country Park, eight miles of wild seacoast set aside and protected. When I visited the park this year, in just a few hours I saw goldfinches, chaffinches, and bramblings in the pine woods, and on the seashore Eurasian wigeons, flocks of oyster-catchers, sandpipers, gulls—and seven human beings.*

Three U.S. presidents especially paid attention to John Muir—Theodore Roosevelt, Woodrow Wilson, and William Howard Taft. While they held office, the United States set aside land for more than 50 national parks, 200 national monuments, and 140 million acres of national forest.

> John Muir was "what few nature lovers are—a man able to influence contemporary thought and action on the subjects to which he had devoted his life...so as to secure the preservation of great natural phenomena—wonderful canyons, giant trees, slopes of flower-spangled hillsides."
>
> —President Theodore Roosevelt, January 1915

Have you heard of Yosemite National Park? Or even visited it? Or the Petrified Forest or the Grand Canyon? Or Mt. Rainier in Washington State, or Sequoia National Park? John Muir personally helped create all those national parks. No wonder he's often called the Father of the U.S. National Park System. And he wasn't even born in the United States!

John Muir was born in Dunbar, Scotland on April 21, 1838. (Congress made April 21, 1988—150 years later—John Muir Day.) When he was eleven, his family moved to the United States. It took their ship six weeks to cross the stormy North Atlantic Ocean.

In Wisconsin, John worked with his brothers from dawn to dark on their father's farm. Their father beat them often. Even when John got mumps and pneumonia, his father made him keep working and refused to call a doctor. John went to college for three years, then he quit to ramble around North America. He worked in sawmills, on farms, in a broom factory, in a carriage factory, and as a sheepherder. When he was twenty-nine, an accident changed his life.

A tool slipped, and a metal spike pierced his right eye. He became totally blind. If he ever could see again, he decided, he would turn his eyes to the fields and woods. In a month, his sight returned, and he set off to walk from Indianapolis to the Gulf of Mexico, 1,000 miles. When he traveled, this time and the many times afterward, he traveled alone, wearing hob-nailed boots. He carried only an old blanket, a hand lens, a pencil and notebook, and for food a bag of hard bread and tea leaves. He never carried a gun.

On this long trip John Muir began to see all of nature as connected. He saw that every rock and plant and human being had its own part to play in the universe, and he began studying the interconnections. After his 1,000-mile walk, he sailed to Cuba, then to Panama, then to San Francisco. He made his home in California for the rest of his life.

> "Around my native town of Dunbar, by the stormy North Sea, there was no lack of wildness.... With red-blooded playmates, wild as myself, I loved to wander in the fields, to hear the birds sing, and along the seashore to gaze and wonder at the shells and seaweeds, eels and crabs in the pools among the rocks when the tide was low."
>
> —John Muir, *The Story of My Boyhood and Youth*

John Muir loved climbing in California's Sierra Nevada mountains. He pioneered what is called "clean climbing" in the United States. He didn't take much equipment when he climbed—no ropes, spikes, or harnesses. He urged everyone to "climb the mountains and get their good tidings." When he helped found a group to guard the environment, he called it the Sierra Club. He hoped the club would "do something for wildness and make the mountains glad."

John Muir taught himself geology and botany. He became an expert on glaciers, an explorer, mountain climber, and teacher. He wrote ten books and hundreds of articles for magazines. More than two hundred sites in the United States have been named in his honor, including the Muir Glacier and Mt. Muir in Alaska and the John Muir Wilderness and the John Muir Trail in the High Sierra.

The Sierra Club Today

The Sierra Club is a nonprofit group that works to save the natural environment. It proposes to:

- Explore, enjoy, and protect the wild places of the earth,
- Use the earth's ecosystems and resources responsibly and encourage others to do that, and
- Teach people to protect and restore the quality of the natural and human environment.

Teenagers high school age and older can join the Sierra Student Coalition. The members explore the planet...work for clean air and water, safe homes, schools, and work places...and work to get good environmental laws passed. Their motto is: *The world is in your hands. Don't drop it.*

THE SIERRA CLUB *helps protect the planet's wild places, so endangered species like this golden eagle can survive.*

BOTTLE GARDENS

SIMPLE BOTTLE GARDEN

THIS TINY ECOSYSTEM YOU CAN MAKE FOR YOUR ROOM STARTS WITH A RECYCLED JAR. RESTAURANTS OFTEN USE VERY LARGE JARS— THEY WILL PROBABLY GIVE YOU ONE IF YOU ASK. IT'S EASIEST IF YOU CAN FIT YOUR HAND IN THE JAR. IF YOU CAN'T, USE STICKS TO PLACE THE PARTS OF YOUR GARDEN WHERE YOU WANT THEM. ONCE YOU'VE CREATED A NEW ECOSYS-TEM, IT'S YOUR JOB TO MAKE SURE IT STAYS HEALTHY—YOU'LL NEED TO BE THE RAINMAKER BY WATERING IT WITH A SPRAY BOTTLE WHEN IT LOOKS DRY.

WHAT YOU NEED

- A large jar with a wide neck
- Clean pebbles and small stones
- Bark from the ground with moss, ivy, or ferns on it
- A spray bottle and water
- If you can't fit your hand in the jar, 2 sticks

WHAT TO DO

1· Collect stones and pebbles from a creek. You can also buy these.

2· Look for interesting bark lying on the ground. If you find bark with moss or small ferns growing on it, soak it in cold water.

3· Be sure your jar is squeaky clean. First put in the pebbles, for drainage. Then place the bark. Take your time deciding how to arrange your ecosystem. If you have moss or ferns growing on your bark, you will soon see drops of moisture on the inside of the glass. Plants give off water, and in this enclosed ecosystem, they can reuse the same water. They still need you to spray them every few days when they get dry.

REEN BOTTLE GARDEN

FOR THIS ECOSYSTEM, YOU'LL ADD MORE PLANTS, SO YOU'LL SEE MORE THINGS GOING ON IN YOUR GARDEN. YOU'LL ALSO NEED TO WATCH IT CAREFULLY TO MAKE SURE THE PLANTS DON'T DRY OUT.

WHAT YOU NEED
- A large jar with a wide neck and a lid, or an old saucer for a top
- Pebbles
- Potting soil from a garden store. You can try dirt from your yard, but potting soil is usually healthier for the plants.
- Small plants and moss from your yard or a garden store—ferns and ivy do well
- Bark and stones if you want them
- A spray bottle and water
- A large spoon
- If you can't fit your hand in the jar, 2 sticks

WHAT TO DO

1. Start with a squeaky clean jar. Cover the bottom with pebbles for drainage. Spoon in the soil. Take your time deciding where you want to put your plants, stones, and bark. Remember that the plants need space to grow.

2. Start at the edges of the jar and make a little hole for each plant. Put the plants in carefully, one at a time. Then place the stones and bark, if you want them in your garden. When you're finished, give the garden a good spray. Cover the top of the jar with a lid or a saucer to keep the water inside. Spray it when it looks dry, at least once a week.

DESERT IN A JAR

FOR CAN CREATE A DESERT ECOSYSTEM AT HOME—NOT WITH COYOTES OR SIDEWINDERS, BUT WITH CACTUS, SAND, AND PEBBLES. LIKE ANY OTHER GROWING THINGS, CACTUSES NEED WATER, SO SPRINKLE A LITTLE ON THE ROCKS WHEN YOU CANNOT SEE ANY DROPS OF WATER ON THE INSIDE OF THE JAR. YOU CAN OFTEN GET SAND FROM A CONSTRUCTION SITE, IF YOU ASK.

WHAT YOU NEED
- A large jar with a lid
- Cactuses from a garden store
- Sand from a garden store or toy store, or ask at a construction site
- Pebbles or small rocks
- A hammer and nail

WHAT TO DO

Follow the directions for the Green Bottle Garden, only add sand instead of soil. After you plant your cactuses, sprinkle in a little water to wet the sand. Make small holes in the lid of the jar with your hammer and nail. Then screw on the lid. Remember to sprinkle in water when there are no water drops on the sides of the jar.

ECO EXTRA

Some desert plants can sprout, flower, and bear seeds in only two weeks. They have to. It may rain in the desert just once a year. The habitats with the greatest variety of wildlife are tropical rain forests, where it rains every day.

How Is a RAIN FOREST Like Your Bathroom?

In a rain forest, guess what happens almost every day? That's right. It rains. So rain forests are very wet and humid. And since the sun shines for 12 hours a day there, they are also very warm. Standing in a rain forest feels a lot like standing in your bathroom after you take a bath. Except you probably don't have orchids and monkeys in your bathroom. All rain forests lie near the equator—in Hawaii, Australia, Asia, Africa, and South America. The largest is in Brazil.

What's Going On?

Rain forests used to cover 20 percent of the earth. Today they cover only 6 percent. Where have the trees gone? People have burned them down so they could plant crops instead, and cut them so they could sell the wood. This is happening very fast. People are burning off more than 4,000 acres of rain forest every hour.

Who Lives in Rain Forests?

Almost as many people live in the rain forests as live in the United States. Besides all the people, half of all the different kinds of plants, animals, birds, and insects in the world live in rain forests—400,000 species. And we think there are at least 9 million species there that we don't know about yet. Some we do know about are:

- Jaguars, ocelots, and deer
- Many kinds of monkeys
- Teak, mahogany, and rosewood trees
- Toucans, parrots, and macaws
- Many varieties of orchids

Why Should You Care?

Since you probably don't live in a rain forest, you might think you don't need to worry about them. But think about this:

- Every day in the rain forest a species becomes extinct. Without help, we will lose one rain forest species every hour.
- One of every four medicines comes from rain forest plants. Scientists believe somewhere among rain forest plants lies the cure for cancer and other diseases. If we destroy the rain forest, we destroy the cures.
- Destroying the rain forests may change the weather all over the world. The earth may become too hot.

What Can You Do?

- Reduce, reuse, and recycle. (You already knew that, right?)
- Talk to people about how important saving the rain forests is.
- Adopt a piece of rain forest through a group like the Nature Conservancy or the National Arbor Day Foundation. (Find out how at the library or on the Internet.)

LEUKEMIA FIGHTER: The rosy periwinkle produces a substance that helps fight leukemia in children.

PAPER QUILTS

THESE QUILTS MAY NOT KEEP YOU TOASTY WARM ON SNOWY NIGHTS, BUT THEY'RE LOTS OF FUN TO MAKE...AND A GREAT WAY TO REUSE PAPER AND SAVE TREES. TRY ANY INTERESTING PAPER—OLD SHEET MUSIC...MAGAZINES AND CATALOGUES...ENDS OF GIFT WRAP AND WALLPAPER. YOU COULD ALSO MAKE SMALL QUILTS FOR SPECIAL GREETING CARDS OR TO DECORATE ALBUMS OR NOTEBOOKS.

WHAT YOU NEED

- Bright paper scraps (You can get books full of wallpaper samples free from wallpaper stores.)
- Poster board or cardboard
- Scissors
- Stick glue
- A ruler
- A pencil and pen
- A homemade marking tool

WHAT TO DO

1· To speed up measuring your quilt pieces, make a marking tool from a scrap of poster board or an old cereal box. Cut a strip about 12" long and exactly 1/16" narrower than you want your quilt squares to be. The 1" squares in the quilts in these photos were made with a marking tool 15/16" wide. If you want 2" squares, make your marking tool 1 15/16" wide.

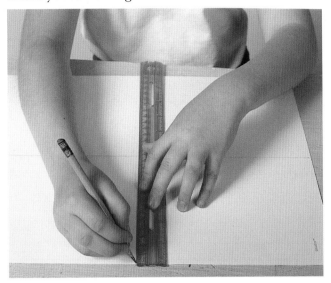

2· Gather all the papers you plan to use, along with pages cut from wallpaper books, magazines, and so on. You can plan your quilt design now if you want to, and pick out colors for that design. Or you can just pick colors you like and plan your design later.

3· Use your marking tool to measure off strips of each paper you want to use. Draw your lines on the back of the paper. The strips need to be right next to each other, so lay your marking tool along one edge of the paper and mark a line along the tool's other side. Now lay the marking tool on the new line and mark a line along the other side. Keep going until you have as many strips as you need.

4· For most quilts, you now turn the paper sideways and repeat drawing strips with your marking tool, so you end up with squares marked out on the back of your paper. For some quilts, like the Notation Quilt in the picture, you use strips that are two or three squares long. Read the directions for the quilt you want to make before you cut. Once you know what shapes you need, cut along the lines. Then organize the squares and strips for each color into piles—an easy way to keep them separate is to put the piles in a muffin tin.

5. If you're not making one of the quilts here, decide what size poster board you want to use and cut it out. Now you can lay out your squares on the poster board and try different patterns to see what you like best. Before you start gluing, mark the center of your poster board. First mark the center of each side, then draw lines connecting the marks on opposite sides—you make a big cross on the poster board, and the center of the cross is the center of the paper. Your quilt will probably turn out straighter if you draw quite a few lines down and across your paper to serve as guidelines. Your poster board will end up looking like a big piece of graph paper.

6. When you glue, it is easier to spread your glue on a section of poster board than on each square. Don't try to glue down more than two or three squares at a time. It's a good idea to start at one corner or in the middle of the paper. To finish your quilt, trim the edges. Attach a string across the back, if you want to hang it up. Or frame it any way you like and then attach a string or wire for hanging.

TO MAKE THE TRIP AROUND THE WORLD QUILT:

This is a traditional quilt pattern. The quilt in the picture uses eight different papers cut in 1" squares and glued on a piece of poster board 11" by 14".

1. Mark the center of your poster board and draw your guidelines. Glue the center of the first square over the center of your poster board, with each corner of the square on a guideline. Work out from the center.

2. At the edges of the poster board, finish with a row of triangles that you make by cutting squares diagonally, from corner to corner.

TO MAKE THE RAINBOW PATH QUILT:

Making quilts by laying patches in diagonal lines is traditional, but copying a rainbow makes this quilt special. The quilt in the picture uses 1" squares in the rainbow's seven colors—red, orange, yellow, green, blue, indigo (blue), and violet. The poster board is 11" by 14". Sometimes two or three shades of a color are laid beside each other before starting the next color.

Mark the center of your poster board and draw your guidelines. Start gluing from the lower left corner and work one row at a time, laying squares diagonally toward the upper right corner.

TO MAKE THE NOTATION QUILT:

Modern quilts often have pieces laid in a pattern that makes a familiar picture, like cats or flowers or—as in this quilt—musical notes. You could make a quilt just like this one or design yours with a different picture.

1· Besides cutting squares, make some strips 2 squares long and some 3 squares long. Mark the center of your poster board and draw your guidelines.

2· Plan how you will lay the squares out. Then shape the tops and bottoms of the notes by taking out parts of the notes—diagonally cut half-squares. Replace them with diagonally cut half-squares of your background design. (If you look at the picture, you can see how to do this.) To make the stems of the notes, cut squares in half.

3· Before you start gluing, mark where you want the border to go along the left side of the poster board and along the bottom. Glue the border squares on last.

4· Begin gluing at the bottom of the quilt, inside the border. Start at the left side and work toward the right. Then glue on the border. Last add the staff lines and flowers.

ATURAL WONDERS: LIP GLOSS, AFTER-BATH POWDER, AND BATH SALTS YOU CAN MAKE FROM NATURE'S MATERIALS... NOTHING ARTIFICIAL, AND EARTH FRIENDLY.

OCEAN WAVES BATH SALTS

Just what you need after a hard day at school, or on the soccer field, or cleaning your room. Drop a handful of your Ocean Waves Bath Salts into a hot tub and relax...or give them to someone else who needs to relax more than you do.

WHAT YOU NEED

- A mixing bowl
- A spoon for mixing
- Measuring spoons
- A whisk or fork
- Blue or green food coloring (unless you want red, for Shell Pink Bath Salts, or yellow, for Sunny Days Bath Salts)
- 1/4 teaspoon of essential oil or perfume oil for fragrance. You can find all kinds of scents at the health food store. (You can add this or not.)
- A jar with a top, washed and dried
- 1 cup of Epsom salts from the grocery store
- 1 cup of sea salt from the grocery store
- 3 tablespoons of dehydrated milk

WHAT TO DO

1· Mix the salts in the mixing bowl.

2· Add eight drops of food coloring and mix it in with the whisk or a fork. If you want it a darker color, add a few more drops of food coloring until you have the color you like.

3· Add the dehydrated milk and mix it in well.

4· If you want your bath salts to have fragrance, mix in the essential oil or perfume now.

5· Be sure your jar is totally dry before you spoon your bath salts into it. Decorate the jar however you like...add a bow...add a label...name it yourself.

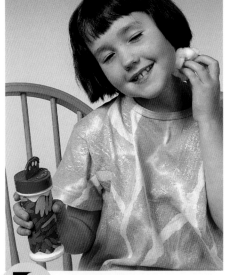

LAVENDER AND ROSES POWDER

Make this sweet-smelling gift for a friend...or dust on your own brand of body powder yourself after a bath or shower. It's easy to make...and all the ingredients are natural. You can get lavender and rose petals at craft stores and health food stores.

WHAT YOU NEED

- A stainless steel, glass, or plastic bowl or other container for mixing
- Measuring cup and spoons
- A whisk or fork
- A recycled glass jar with a tight-fitting lid for storing
- A coffee filter
- A bit of string
- An electric blender or a mortar and pestle
- 1½ cups of corn starch
- ½ cup of baking soda
- 3 tablespoons of lavender flowers
- 2 tablespoons of rose petals
- 1 teaspoon of cloves
- 1 teaspoon of ground cinnamon or a cinnamon stick
- 1 teaspoon of dried lemon or orange peel

WHAT TO DO

1· Mix the cornstarch and baking soda together in the bowl with your whisk or fork.

2· Grind the lavender and rose petals in the blender or by hand with the mortar and pestle, until they are powder.

3· Add the flower powder to the bowl. Mix again.

4· Make a fragrance packet. Put the cloves, cinnamon, and orange or lemon peel in the center of the coffee filter. Tie with a string to make a pouch.

5· Put the pouch in the bottom of your jar. Carefully scoop the mixture from your bowl on top of it. Put the lid on the jar and put the jar in a brown bag for at least two weeks.

6· After two or three weeks, open the jar and remove the pouch. Your powder is ready to use. You can decorate the jar and add a pretty powder puff... or put the powder in a recycled shaker...or punch holes in the jar lid to make it into a shaker...or come up with your own idea for packaging.

7· You may want to add a ribbon or make a label with the name of your special powder on it.

LEMONADE LIP GLOSS

You can go pretty wild with this all-natural lip gloss recipe. Pick the color, pick the flavor, decorate the label...and name it yourself. Cocolicious Coconut? Bananafana? Aren't Ya Orange? Gorilla Vanilla? Well, maybe not.

WHAT YOU NEED

- A small pan and a glass measuring cup or a double boiler
- Measuring spoons
- Reused lip balm tube or small pot
- 3 tablespoons of almond or olive oil
- 1 tablespoon of beeswax from a health food store
- 1/4 teaspoon of flavoring, such as lemon, orange, vanilla, strawberry...
- Food coloring
- For labels—gift wrap or fabric scraps, paper, glue, colored pens

WHAT TO DO

Before you start, wash your old lip balm tube or little pot with warm soapy water. You may want to soak these overnight to remove labels.

1· Put two or three cups of water in the bottom of your double boiler or in your small pan. Measure the almond or olive oil and the beeswax into the top of the double boiler, or in your glass measuring cup.

2· Ask an adult to help you heat the pan over medium heat until the beeswax melts, and to take the pan off the stove.

3· Let the wax cool for a minute or two. Then add the flavoring and two or three drops of food coloring.

4· Carefully pour the liquid into the glass measuring cup or any container with a pouring lip. Then pour from the measuring cup into the empty tube or little pot. Don't move the tube or pot for at least fifteen minutes, until the lip gloss is cool.

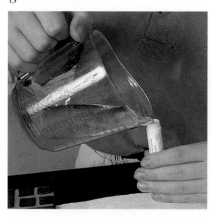

5· Make your label and decorate with gift wrap or fabric, or colored pens...whatever works for you!

COOL TOOL
Make an Earth-Friendly Art Box

You know from experience that you can make really neat things with ordinary stuff from around your house—like collages and puppets and costumes. And you've probably noticed that you can make most of the projects in this book from ordinary stuff, too. Mostly from things you reuse, like cans and magazines. You can make even more interesting projects if you start collecting and saving all kinds of materials. Tin cans, for instance. And buttons. And calendars.

When you start a project, wouldn't it be great to have all the supplies on hand? And in one place? How about making a big art box, maybe from a cardboard box, to store all your art supplies in? You could decorate it, or you could just write "**ART BOX**" on it in big letters, so no one will use it for anything else.

Some things to collect just for the projects in this book (of course you'll wash them first, if they need it—otherwise you'll find yourself with an interesting collection of bugs and blue mossy gunk and nose-pinching smells):

- cereal boxes
- tin cans
- yogurt, cottage cheese, and milk cartons
- buttons, fabric scraps, ribbon, yarn
- old plates, broken pots
- beads, screws, nails
- jars, bottles, jar tops
- brown grocery bags
- newspaper, magazines, calendars, catalogues
- parts of old board games
- egg cartons, frozen dinner trays

You get the idea. The next time you can't think of anything to do, take a look at your Art Box for inspiration. And remind yourself what an awesome earth-saver you are.

TIN CAN MARIONETTE

- Tin cans! With their top and bottom lids still on. The marionette in the picture uses these sizes: 1 soup can for head, 1 large juice can for body, 6 evaporated milk cans for arms and thighs, 2 dog food cans for legs, 2 cat food cans for feet
- Bubble wrap
- A mesh orange or grapefruit bag for hair
- Old hardware—screws, nuts, bolts, chain
- A roll of strong wire
- Pop tops
- Scraps of gold gift wrap and ribbon, buttons
- A paper plate
- A plastic cup
- 1 piece of plastic pipe or paper towel roll, about 3"
- 2 pieces of plastic pipe or paper towel roll, about 8" each
- A hot glue gun
- A hammer and nail
- An old wooden yardstick or scraps of wood for the controls
- Fishing line
- A Sharp knife
- Aluminum foil

WHAT TO DO

1· If they're not already empty, drain your cans by punching their tops with a punch-type can opener or with a hammer and nail. Take one end off the dog food cans.

WHEN FORESTS COVERED THE WORLD, MARIONETTES WERE MADE OF WOOD. TODAY, A GREAT WAY YOU CAN CONSERVE WOOD AND RECYCLE AT THE SAME TIME IS TO MAKE MARIONETTES OUT OF...TIN CANS! AND POP TOPS, SCRAPS OF BUBBLE WRAP AND ALUMINUM FOIL... A MESH ORANGE BAG...ALL KINDS OF ODDS AND ENDS.

2. To put your marionette together, you're going to thread wire through holes in the cans. Look at the drawing to see where to punch holes with a hammer and nail to thread the wire through.

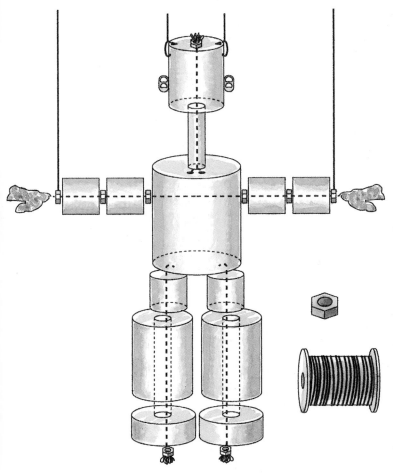

- For the soup can head, a hole in the center of the top and bottom. Two holes on each side at the top to attach the control wires.

- For each milk can, holes in the center of the top and bottom.

- For the large juice can body: Four holes in the bottom—two at the top of each leg. Two holes in the top for the neck. One hole toward the top of each side for the arm wires.

- For each dog food can leg, a hole in the top.

- For each cat food can foot, a hole toward the back of the top.

3. Lay your cans and pieces of pipe out on a table in the shape of the marionette. Look at the drawing to be sure of what goes where.

4. Starting at the top, thread your wire through the soup can, then through the 3" pipe neck. Hook the end through the two holes in the top of the juice can body, and cut the wire off. On top of the head, cut the other end of your wire, leaving about 14". Make that 14" into a coil or bunch and secure it by screwing a nut in the hole at the top of the head.

5. To attach the arms, thread fishing line straight through two milk cans, then through the juice can, then through the other two milk cans. Leave enough line at each end to attach hands. Shape the hands from wire and wrap aluminum foil around them.

6. To attach the legs and feet, start at the feet. Leave enough wire at the bottom to wrap around a nut, to keep the wire from pulling through the hole. Run your wire through one foot, one long piece of pipe, and one milk can. Hook the end through one set of holes in the bottom of the juice can body, and cut the wire off. Do the same thing for the other leg.

7. Ask an adult to help you hot glue the neck pipe to the head and the body, and hot glue the milk cans and feet to the leg pipes.

8. Now add all the special decoration you want to. The marionette in the picture has an orange mesh bag glued on for hair, bubble wrap for a skirt, buttons for eyes and nose, and a chain necklace. Her hat is a part of a plastic cup and bubble wrap glued on a paper plate. Her ears are pop tops.

TO MAKE THE CONTROLS

Look at the drawing of the controls as you follow these directions. You need two pieces of yardstick or scrap wood each about 9½" long, and one piece about 14" long. In the drawing, the short pieces are 2 and 3. The long piece is 1.

1· Glue one short piece to the middle of the long piece. This is marked X in the drawing.

2· With a sharp knife, make notches in this short piece on either side of the long piece. These notches are marked A and B in the drawing. Make notches toward each end of the other short piece. These are marked C and D. These notches are where you will wrap the control wires.

3· You need four control wires, or lines. Look at the drawing to see how to wrap them. When you wrap the wire on the controls and hook the ends through the head, you need to have about 12" of wire between the head and your controls. You need about 30" of wire between each wrist and your controls.

4· To make your marionette wave, walk, dance, and sit down, you hold stick 3 in one hand and the cross (sticks 1 and 2) in the other hand.

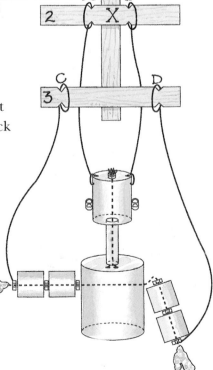

Adopt a Piece of THE PLANET

Somewhere nearby lies a bit of the Earth that needs your help. Maybe it's a place you pass on your way to school. Or in your neighborhood. Or in your own yard. Maybe your school would let you and some friends adopt a part of your schoolyard.

What can you do when you find a bit of land to adopt?
- Pick up litter.
- Plant some grass, seeds, or seedling plants to make the soil healthy again.
- Plant some flowers.
- Plant some bushes or trees to make a habitat for squirrels and birds.
- Hang up a bird feeder, a birdhouse, or a birdbath.

Another way to adopt a piece of the planet is to write to a group that is protecting endangered ecosystems. That way you help save special lands and the animals, birds, and plants that live there. For instance, you can adopt a piece of rain forest through the Nature Conservancy, the National Arbor Day Foundation, and other groups (page 126). You can find their addresses on the Internet and at the library.

BISON *are an endangered species, and so is their home, the tallgrass prairie. You can adopt an acre of tallgrass prairie through the Nature Conservancy.*

BEAN AND PASTA MOSAIC

YOU CAN MAKE MOSAICS FROM JUST ABOUT ANYTHING YOU CAN GLUE DOWN—BITS OF PAPER, PEBBLES, BEACH GLASS, OR BEANS AND PASTA LIKE THE ONE HERE. USE ANY KIND OF BEANS AND ANY KIND OF PASTA. DEPENDING ON WHAT YOU CHOOSE FOR YOUR BASE, YOU CAN ALSO MAKE MOSAIC JEWELRY OR DECORATE OLD BOXES OR COOKIE TINS.

WHAT YOU NEED

- Beans and pasta
- White glue or glue stick
- Corrugated cardboard, a jar lid, a box, or whatever you want for a base
- A pencil and paper
- Paint and a paintbrush if you need them

WHAT TO DO

1· Paint your base, if you want to.

2· You can draw your design on a piece of paper. Or you can draw it right on your base. Or you can design your mosaic as you go along. Or you can lay out your beans and pasta on a piece of paper and transfer the design a little at a time to your base. You may find the easiest way to plan your design is to start at the center.

3· Glue on your beans and pasta in the design you have planned.

It Is Always Sunrise Somewhere

When we contemplate the globe as one great dewdrop,
   striped and dotted with continents and islands,
   flying through space with all the other stars,
   all singing and shining together as one,
    the whole universe appears as an infinite storm of beauty.

This grand show is eternal.
   It is always sunrise somewhere.
     The dew is never all dried at once.
       A shower is forever falling, vapor forever rising.

Eternal sunrise, eternal sunset,
   eternal dawn and gloaming,
   on seas and continents and islands,
   each in its turn, as the round earth rolls.

—John Muir, *My First Summer in the Sierra*

Project Designers

EVANS CARTER (twig frame, paper beads, seed mosaic) creates art and order in Asheville, North Carolina, at home and at Lark Books.

MAYA CONTENTO (potato print t-shirts, print gift wrap, calendar boxes, paper bag books) styles food, cooks gourmet meals, and designs shirts in Asheville, North Carolina.

KATHY COOPER (collecting bag) is the author of *The Complete Book of Floorclothes* (Lark Books). She and her daughter **SUNNY**, 7½, who drew the design for the bag in this book, live and play in King, North Carolina.

JAN COPE (collection box, log cabin planter, wetland, gardens in a jar, painted flowerpots) loves creative projects, and frequently redesigns her garden, her house, and her life.

CINDY CRANDALL-FRAZIER (paper quilts) wrote *Sock Doll Workshop* (Lark Books) and taught herself art and design. She has a big paper quilt on her dining room wall in Williamsburg, Virginia.

Mural artist **ROLF HOLMQUIST** (bat house, bird feeder, dog biscuit frame) is building a house full of beautiful old wood in Micaville, North Carolina.

JUDY HORN (cornhusk angels, sunflowers, bag bouquets) owns the Cornhusk Shoppe in Weaverville, North Carolina, where she creates wonderful wreaths and other items from... cornhusks.

LIZ HUGHEY (sand candles, nature's garden bottles, decoupage bottles) draws beautiful flowers and colorful designs on everything in Gainesville, Florida, except her latest major creation, a baby boy.

A book designer at Lark Books, **DANA IRWIN** (marionette, chair, bird) has been a creative artist since birth, and probably before.

ELAINE KNOLL (gourd birdhouse and witch) transforms gourds into all kinds of art in Leicester, North Carolina.

Swannanoa, North Carolina, artist **NANCY MCGAHA** (eggshell mosaic) beads elegant vests and smocks natural clothing...and of course eats lots of eggs.

DEBBIE MIDKIFF (powder, lip balm, bath salts) owns the Weed Patch in Barboursville, West Virginia, where she concocts all kinds of natural products for people and animals.

In Coon Rapids, Minnesota, **JULIE PETERSON** (birch bark canoe, basket) designs kits and finished products from birch bark and other natural materials. For a list, send a self-addressed legal size envelope to Minnesota Naturals, 10291 Mississippi Blvd., Coon Rapids, MN 55433.

When he isn't creating beautiful mosaics and paper art from objects he uncovers at flea markets and antique stores, **TERRY TAYLOR** (achy breaky pots, recycled albums, beach glass jewelry, nature journal) wanders the world seeking books and art for the Lark Books catalog.

An accomplished potter and visual artist, **PAMELLA WILSON** (clay pots, kiln, piñata, bag bonnets, puppets, rock houses) also shines at the art of friendship in Asheville, North Carolina.

Metric Conversion Table

LENGTH

- To convert inches to centimeters,
  multiply the number of inches by 2.5.

- To convert feet to meters,
  divide the number of feet by 3.25.

INCHES	CM	INCHES	CM
⅛	.5	12	31
¼	1	13	33.5
⅜	1.25	14	36
½	1.5	15	38.5
⅝	1.75	16	41
¾	2	17	44
⅞	2.25	18	46
1	2.5	19	49
1¼	3.5	20	51
1½	4	21	54
1¾	4.5	22	56.5
2	5	23	59
2½	6.5	24	62
3	8	25	64
3½	9	26	67
4	10	27	69
4½	11.5	28	72
5	13	29	74.5
5½	14	30	77
6	15	31	79.5
7	18	32	82
8	21	33	85
9	23	34	87
10	26	35	90
11	28	36	92.5

VOLUME

1 fluid ounce		29.6 ml
1 pint		473 ml
1 quart		946 ml
1 gallon		3.785 l

"Winter will pass, the days will lengthen, the ice will melt in the pasture pond. The song sparrow will return and sing, the frogs will awake, the warm wind will blow again. All these sights and sounds and smells will be yours to enjoy, Wilbur—this lovely world, these precious days...."

—E. B. White, *Charlotte's Web*

Index